ORIGINS *of* STORY

ORIGINS *of* STORY

ON WRITING FOR CHILDREN

❧

EDITED BY

BARBARA HARRISON

and

GREGORY MAGUIRE

❧

MARGARET K. McELDERRY BOOKS

Every effort has been made by the editors and publisher to
locate all persons having any rights or interests in the material
published in this book. Any existing rights not acknowledged
herein will, if the editor or publisher is notified, be duly
acknowledged in future editions of this book.

Margaret K. McElderry Books
An imprint of Simon & Schuster Children's Publishing Division
1230 Avenue of the Americas
New York, New York 10020

Book design by Michael Nelson
The text of this book is set in Cochin.

Printed in the United States of America

10 9 8 7 6 5 4 3 2

Library of Congress Cataloging-in-Publication Data
Origins of story: on writing for children / edited by Barbara Harrison and
Gregory Maguire. — 1st ed.   p.   cm.
Summary: Collection of 17 lectures originally presented at programs and
lectures sponsored by Children's Literature New England.
ISBN 0-689-82604-4
1. Children's literature — Authorship. I. Harrison, Barbara, 1936-
II. Maguire, Gregory. III. Children's Literature New England.
PN147.5.075   1999   808.06'8 — dc21   98-45300

FIRST
EDITION

In memory of Paul and Ethel Heins

CONTENTS

ACKNOWLEDGMENTS

We would like to thank past and present board members of Children's Literature New England. They include Virginia Golodetz, Betty Levin, Jill Paton Walsh, Barbara Scotto, John Rowe Townsend, and Martha Walke.

Children's Literature New England relies on the help of a stalwart band of friends and companions. There are more people than can be named here. We hope it will suffice to remark that our eleventh annual institute, called *Looking for the Village: The Child and Community,* could only have been possible because we have already found the village. It is you.

—Barbara Harrison and Gregory Maguire

INTRODUCTION

✑

We are the stories we tell, the fictions we spin, each of us experiencing countless beginnings and endings, births and rebirths, within the context of our lives.

Under the aegis of Children's Literature New England (CLNE), a nonprofit educational organization founded in 1987, individuals have met annually on university campuses on both sides of the Atlantic to discuss books remarkable in narrative structure as well as in their insight into children's lives. The essays in *Origins of Story* represent some of the themes of programs sponsored by CLNE, themes chosen to reflect vital concerns of children as expressed in the books written for them.

Implicit in the essays is the realization that we have much to learn from literature that mirrors the lives of children. Children, as Jill Paton Walsh reminds us, live in a different relation to the flow of time. For children, story is as new as experience itself; indeed, the best of stories for children contain something of the freshness of childhood. When children's writers are wise in the ways of the world, they anticipate the freshness of their audience and they reserve for children the choicest of material—what Walter de la Mare called "the rarest kind of best."

In *Origins of Story*, notable writers for children consider how literature, memory, and moral passion serve the writer. The contributing authors reach beyond themselves and their work to discuss home and homelessness, violence and nonviolence, the nature—or natures—of heroism. The contributors assert that the best of stories for children are, in the words of Katherine Paterson, metaphors to live by.

Through the years, the programs of Children's Literature New England have been an affirmation of the vital connection between children's books and the imagination. With themes like Swords and Ploughshares, Homecoming, Worlds Apart, and Endings and Beginnings, CLNE's institutes become a clarion call on behalf of childhood itself. At the heart of each exploration—both the institute theme and the individual pieces here collected—is the belief that the best of literature unriddles the world, encourages reflection, and deepens appreciation for both the peril and the promise of life.

—Barbara Harrison and Gregory Maguire

ORIGINS *of* STORY

UP THE BEANSTALK

GILLIAN CROSS

When I was a child, I was always puzzled by the heroic status accorded to Jack, who climbed the beanstalk. Alone among the fairy-tale heroes, he was plainly undeserving. Cinderella suffered sweetly in the kitchen, to win her right to shine at the ball. The Sleeping Beauty was kind and generous, even if those qualities were given to her by magic. Dick Whittington was persevering, and Tom Thumb triumphed over the problems of his small stature. But Jack was lazy and stupid, and all he did was climb the beanstalk and steal treasures from a giant who had never done him any harm.

All he did was climb the beanstalk. . . .

I see things a little differently now. When I think of Jack, I see him poised at the bottom of the huge, spreading beanstalk, broad leaves rustling all around him, and one foot on the first twisting spiral of the thick stems. He stands, and he looks upwards, to where the beanstalk disappears into a blanket of dense white cloud. And he thinks—what does he think? What would *you* think, in that situation, not knowing what lay at the top of that strange green pillar? I don't suppose there is a single one of us who can remember the first time she heard the tale of Jack and the Beanstalk. Who can recall the delicious terror of climbing with Jack and discovering, at precisely the same moment as he does, that eerie land above the clouds?

But Jack does more than discover that land. By his entry into it, he creates it, out of nothing, for if he had not climbed the beanstalk, there would have been no land at all. In fiction, at least, Bishop Berkeley rules: The tree in the quad cannot exist in any of those worlds apart, unless someone has occasion to look at it. And the existence of any fictional world is dependent on there being a narrator who sets out to find it. It can be created by a few strokes of the pen, or a few words from the story-teller, but if the story-teller is silent and the pen is still, it is without form and void. Nothing will come into being until the narrator lifts that last supporting foot from the ground, leaving behind everything that *exists already*.

And that is a hard thing to do.

People who are not story-tellers imagine that the difficulty is a different one. "How do you get your ideas?" they say, as though, once the idea is formed (and they imagine that as a technical process, like building a bridge out of Meccano), the narrating of the story is merely a necessary formality.

But ideas are ten a penny. Standing at the bottom of the beanstalk, I can look up into the clouds and imagine a hundred lands above the clouds. Blue and green and yellow lands. Lands full of bubbles, or rocking horses, or monkeys typing the works of Shakespeare. The beanstalk could lead to any or all of those, for I can invent what I like about the view above the cumulus.

But simply getting the *idea* for a fictional world does not make it exist. The narrator has to launch himself forward into it. Like Jack, he must summon up the energy and courage to take the first step. To lift his foot from the ground and trust to a staircase that might lead anywhere—or nowhere. Whatever incantations we chant, whatever rituals we perform, we cannot enter a world apart without letting go of this one.

That was a lesson I had to learn when I began to write. Before I began my second book—which was my first real one— I sat down to make full and detailed notes. I thought that that was what writers did. Fresh from finishing a doctoral thesis, I was accustomed to pulling information together and organizing it in elegant, logical structures that would enable people to take an overview of three years of research in the space of sixty thousand words or so. Naturally, I imagined that writing a novel of sixty thousand words or so must be a similar process, and I set myself to apply my newly acquired skills to this slightly different field.

My intended book was set in the rural south of England, in the nineteenth century, a time and place about which I already knew a fair amount. But I wasn't just trying to take advantage of my reading to put together some kind of story. What I wanted was much more complicated, although I don't think I realized that at the time. I wanted to experience, directly, the quality of nineteenth-century English life. I wanted to make a world for myself out of what I had read. "We cannot get into the forest of the past," says C. S. Lewis. "That is what the word *past* means." But I didn't believe him. I was walking the same ground that nineteenth-century Sussex people trod. I knew the shape of their hills and the limits of their villages. I knew what they ate, what they wore, how they fed their babies, what jobs they did, what diseases they died of and—to the last, pitiful penny—how they spent their money. If I only drew together all that knowledge, I would be able (or so I thought) to feel what it must have been like to *be* one of those villagers of 150 years ago. I walked on the Downs above my house, beside that windmill base that had been made into a cottage, and longed to hear the creak of the long-vanished windmill sails, turning somewhere above my head. And it seemed to me that if only I organized what I knew, I would achieve an emotional and imaginative and *perceptual* overview that would be as real and immediate as the creak of the windmill sails.

So I made notes.

I took a new, clean ring-backed notebook and I headed up the pages with broad, simple categories that represented all the things I thought I should know before I worked out the story I was going to tell. I still have the notebook somewhere, and the headings are as clearly written as ever.

WHAT DID THEY WEAR?
WHAT DID THEY EAT?
HOW DID THEY TALK?
HOW DID THEY SPEND THEIR TIME?

All very clear and comprehensive.

But underneath, the pages are pristine. As white and blank as they were when I first bought the book. There is not a single word entered under any of my careful headings.

Because the headings, by themselves, were too much for me to bear. I can still remember the leaden despair that overtook me when I realized exactly how much information each heading represented. It was not the idea of finding it out that was daunting. I was, after all, used to research, and I enjoy the detailed hunting for obscure pieces of information. What paralyzed me was the sheer imaginative efforts that would have been needed to pull all that information together into a coherent picture.

Weighed down by all that, how could I tell a story? How could I advance my characters a step, if I had to check for Historical Correctness at the end of every sentence? You only have to consider a single action properly, to see how impossible it would have been. Imagine, let us say, a book that opens with a ten-year-old boy running out to play with his friend one Sunday the ninth of November 1842.

But—*was* the ninth of November a Sunday? And if it was, what significance would that have had for the son of a poor agricultural laborer in East Sussex? Would he have been to church beforehand? Or chapel? Would he have been wearing his best clothes? His old clothes? His only clothes? Was he free to play, or would he have been feeding pigs and chickens, or scaring birds away from the Squire's corn? When he saw his friend (whom he had known since they were born, and expected to know for the rest of his life), would he feel differently from a modern child (who moves between houses and schools, and who continually has to present himself to strangers, and to establish his identity and those of the people around him)? Could *friend* have the same meaning in that different context?

The questions are only just beginning, and the boy hasn't even launched his first kick at the football (would they have had a football?). It would take a whole adult novel to begin to understand who he is and how he feels as he aims that kick. A novel with a complex, teasing structure, and much intellectual discourse about the problems of historicity. Without ever advancing beyond the boy running out into the sunshine (or was it rain? or fog?), one could achieve a startling imaginative evocation of the distance between us and that moment of 150 years ago. If one of you cares to write such a book, I will read it with great pleasure and interest.

But I don't long for it to exist, and I didn't long for anything like that in the moment, nearly twenty years ago now, when I sat staring down at my blank notebook. What I longed for was to *be there,* in the forest of the past, hearing the leaves rustle and smelling the wet, dank smell of the moss.

Only I'd just proved that that was impossible. Hadn't I? I was poised, like Jack at the bottom of the beanstalk, staring up at the clouds above and realizing that, however hard I plied my telescope, I was never going to be able to work out what lay behind that insubstantial, impenetrable barrier. From where I was, there was no way of getting a grip on where I wanted to be.

Except for the beanstalk.

I did have my own version of that. Nothing like as grand and solid as Jack's. Just a thin, wispy, mental picture of a poor country boy on top of a hill. I didn't know who he was or where he came from, but I could feel the ground underneath him, and the excitement he felt as he lay gazing down at hundreds of navvies who were laboring, with spades and wheelbarrows, to build an embankment for the new railway to London. He was my starting point.

I understood, of course, that the picture appealed to me because it seemed to sum up the Victorian age, with all its staggering contrasts and changes and opportunities. Intellectually, I realized that the boy was a good place to begin my story, and I had assumed that, once my notes were made and my plot was planned, I would know all about him, and what was going to happen to him. When I abandoned the notes, I expected the boy to vanish too. How could he be real when I couldn't get a grip on his world?

But he didn't vanish. He went on lying there, gazing down, with his mouth open and his arms resting on the grass under his head. And, as if I were sleepwalking, I picked up my pen, took my last foot off the ground, and began to write:

Grrr-on!
    A huge hand thudded down, knocking a cloud of chalky dust from the horse's rump, and the animal lumbered into a trot along the

embankment. The navvy holding the bridle ran beside, while the loaded truck gathered speed as it swayed faster and faster after them.

Whoa there!

The swerve came like magic, man and horse turning aside in a single practiced moment.

CRASH!

With a rattle of earth and rocks the truck bumped the log across the unfinished end of the embankment, tipped up and thundered its load down the slope.

Jem let out his breath and wriggled forward on his stomach to stick his head even farther out of the bushes.

That was it. I was away up the beanstalk of narrative, drawn on by the simple logic of the ascending spirals. And when I stepped into the strange land at the top, I was looking not at nineteenth-century England, but at a particular boy in a particular place. Jem's village was not just any village, drawn to fit in with the statistics I had read. It was the village where Joe Hamage was blacksmith and meddlesome Mrs. Neville was the vicar's wife. When Jem left the embankment, he walked back to a broken home (broken for the good nineteenth-century reasons that his mother was dead in childbirth, and his father was transported for poaching to Van Diemen's Land), but it was not a typical nineteenth-century teenage sister that he found there. It was—Kate. Poor, proud Kate, with the sharp elbows and the sweet singing voice and the terrible, sour temper.

I didn't cast all my historical knowledge to the winds. The appropriate details came to my mind when they were necessary, just as the scalpel arrives in the surgeon's hand when he needs it. And if the details didn't come, I went and looked them up, but I never thought much about them, any more than the surgeon thinks about his equipment while he is using it. I was concentrating on Kate and Jem Penfold, and the particular nature of the claustrophobic, suspicious village where they lived and the tragedy that it produced. When I realized what the end of my story had to be, I was surprised and regretful, but I knew that there was no evading it. It was inevitable, by the laws of the world I was inhabiting.

The curious thing is that, when I step back and contemplate it now, that book, *The Iron Way*, with its emotional story and its tragic denouement, does seem to epitomize my feelings about that period of history. The relationship between Kate and Conor O'Brien, the navvy whom she loves and who presents her with a chance of escape that is cruelly snatched away, could be seen as a paradigm of the immediate results of the Industrial Revolution in England. The technological developments of that period could have meant—and ultimately did mean—a major improvement in the circumstances of ordinary people. But in the short term, they caused a great deal of conflict and misery, as people tried to cope with changes that were outside their control. I am entertained to think that, by accident, I landed up doing what I had set out to do. That I managed, somehow, to construct a whole imaginative world out of my tantalizing accumulated knowledge.

But it was not what I was trying to do while I wrote. From the moment I began to concentrate on Jem Penfold watching the navvies, I forgot all about making historical pictures. The world at the end of the railway embankment was a separate reality, with its own distinctive flavor. It simply happened to share certain characteristics of nineteenth-century England.

I have told this story at some length, not because I think there is anything exceptional about the book I was then writing, but because I think my experience is typical of the whole process of entering the "world apart" of the story-teller. Every world that lives with us, after we first read about it, has been explored by someone who *did not know what was there beforehand*, who climbed like Jack (and like the first narrator of Jack's story) not only in ignorance, but also without knowing, for sure, that there was anything at all above the clouds.

In some books, traces of that are clearly visible. What works on the readers is the very mechanism which first worked on the writer, and I think it is worth looking at that. Consider, for example, *The Secret Garden*. There can be few moments more magical than the one in which Mary Lennox opens the hidden door under the ivy and first gains entry to that world-within-a-world that has been locked up for ten years:

> She put her hands under the leaves and began to pull and push them aside. Thick as the ivy hung, it nearly all was a loose and swinging curtain, though some had crept over wood and iron. Mary's heart began to thump and her hands to shake a little in her delight and excitement. The robin kept singing and twittering away and tilting his head on one side, as if he were as excited as she was. What was this thing under her hands which was square and made of iron and which her fingers found a hole in?
>
> It was the lock of the door which had been closed ten years, and she put her hand in her pocket, drew out the key, and found it fitted the keyhole. She put the key in and turned it. It took two hands to do it, but it did turn.
>
> And then she took a long breath and looked behind her up the long walk to see if anyone was coming. No one was coming. No one ever did

come, it seemed, and she took another long breath, because she could not help it, and she held back the swinging curtain of ivy and pushed back the door which opened slowly—slowly.

Then she slipped through it, and shut it behind her and stood with her back against it, looking about her and breathing quite fast with excitement, and wonder, and delight.

She was standing inside the secret garden.

Anyone reading that for the first time must experience a most delicious mixture of anticipation and curiosity. The world of *The Secret Garden* is a world of forbidden places, of closed rooms and secret knowledge, and at the heart of them all lies the garden. It is, in every sense, the key to the story, providing both explanation and cure for the mysteries of Misselthwaite Manor. And, at the same time, it is itself the most desirable place in the book: a symbol of Spring and renewal; the epitome of wholesome, natural beauty; the object of Mary's nurturing and a place where she can, herself, develop in safety.

But once it did not exist. And what I have just read you is, I believe, a beanstalk passage. An incantation, with which the author conjured herself into the center of her imagined world. When we read the story for the first time, we may not know what lies behind the hidden door in the wall, but we know that there is *something*. The mere shape of the book tells us that. Four-fifths of it still lie ahead of us, in a reassuring slab of pages, and we can give ourselves up to anticipation and curiosity, secure in the knowledge that there is a secret to be discovered behind the door.

But Frances Hodgson Burnett did not have that comforting knowledge. However much she believed in that garden, and knew it was there, she could not experience it unless she took her foot off the ground and conjured herself through the locked door. Look at the description of how Mary inserts the key and turns it; it is more detailed and slow-moving than almost anything else in the book.

> . . . she put her hand in her pocket, drew out the key, and found it fitted the keyhole. She put the key in and turned it. It took two hands to do it, but it did turn.
>
> And then she took a long breath and looked behind her up the long walk to see if anyone was coming. No one was coming. No one ever did come, it seemed, and she took another long breath, because she could not help it, and she held back the swinging curtain of ivy and pushed back the door which opened slowly—slowly.

I don't think that detail is an accident. Nor do I think it is simply a device to prolong suspense for the reader. I think it is the way in which Frances Hodgson Burnett evoked, for herself, the reality of her imagined world. And that is how she opened the mysterious door—and *saw*.

What she saw, of course, was not the crudely symbolic garden that I have sketched above, but a real and particular garden, with an atmosphere like no other.

> It was the sweetest, most mysterious-looking place anyone could imagine. The high walls which shut it in were covered with the leafless stems of climbing roses, which were so thick that they were matted together. . . . There were other trees in the garden, and one of the things which made the place look strangest and loveliest was

that climbing roses had run all over them and swung down long tendrils which made light swaying curtains, and here and there they had caught at each other or at a far-reaching branch and had crept from one tree to another and made lovely bridges of themselves. There were neither leaves nor roses on them now, and Mary did not know whether they were dead or alive, but their thin grey or brown branches and sprays looked like a sort of hazy mantle spreading over everything, walls, and trees, and even brown grass, where they had fallen from their fastenings and run along the ground. . . .

We could all construct, I am sure, some kind of explanation of the emotional significance of the garden. A garden is a symbol as old as Genesis and the *hortus conclusus*—the enclosed garden—is one of the clichés of Christian art, representing the beauty of chastity. Then there is the rose run wild. The branches which look dead until the spring wakes them. The silence that is as old as Mary herself. It's tempting to play around with all those notions.

But none of them will explain the truly striking thing about the garden, or about the book. What we remember is the particular reality of Misselthwaite Manor, and the moor, and those indomitable growing things. I love gardens. My own gives me enormous pleasure, and I never miss an opportunity to visit those of other people. But, with one exception, that walled enclosure at Misselthwaite Manor is more real to me than any garden I have ever seen. Each spring, the fat green spikes of crocus leaves, pushing their way through the earth, seem *almost* as real as the sharp, pale green points that Mary Lennox finds when she first penetrates the locked door. And the seed packets in the supermarkets seem to hold the promise of Dickon's mignonette and poppies as'll come up and bloom if you just whistle to 'em. The secret garden is not a parable. It is sharply visualized and vividly alive. Any other significance it owns has accrued to it almost by accident, as a natural result of its triumphant reality.

Maybe the process that I have just outlined seems far-fetched and unlikely to you, but I am bold to put forward my theory because what I see in that passage in *The Secret Garden* parallels what has happened to me many times, most notably when I was writing *Wolf*.

When I embarked on that book, I had no more than the haziest idea of what it was about, or what was going to happen. I knew simply that Cassy was sent away from her Nan's flat, because of a mysterious visitor who arrived at night, and that the story was, in some way I could not work out properly, deeply involved with wolves.

So I began to climb. I got Cassy out of Nan's flat and sent her scurrying round London until she discovered the squat where Goldie, her mother, was staying. I had her talk her way into the squat and realize that her mother was upstairs—and then I knew that my flannelling time had run out. I had to *get into* the particular and peculiar world of that book, or it would never work.

So I did just what Frances Hodgson Burnett did. I thought myself into the place where Cassy was, concentrating on the details:

> Cassy walked slowly down the hall, still carrying her suitcase. It was too dark to see much, but the house had the cave-like smell of mold. The tiles felt broken and uneven under her feet and when she touched the wall loose plaster crumbled away from her fingers.

All her life she had been coming to visit Goldie in places like this. Places with greasy floors and cobwebby ceilings, where smells hung on the stairs and the corners were clogged with dirt. But she had always come with Nan before. And with Nan's scouring powder and scrubbing brush and disinfectant, ready to clean everything up. This time it was different.

She climbed the stairs, plodding heavily from step to step, heading for the light that shone, very faintly, onto the landing. It was coming from the room on her right, at the back of the house. Heaving her case another couple of feet, Cassy tapped lightly on the door.

Come in!

That was Goldie's voice, giggly and excited. Cassy pushed the door open—

—and as she did it, I *knew* what she saw behind the door. I entered the room at the same moment as she did, and to begin with I saw it simply as an extraordinary place:

It was like . . . an infinite forest, full of fireflies. The darkness flickered with points of flame that dipped and swelled all round [Cassy], retreating endlessly. . . . The room had no limits. Left and right, behind and in front and above, the lights and the flowers surrounded her with patterns that destroyed her sense of space. The shock of it froze her brain and she gripped the handle of her suitcase, standing completely still as she worked out where the boundaries were.

It took her more than a minute. Slowly she

realized that she was looking at reflections. . . .

Goldie was sitting on a mattress in one corner, as still and upright as a doll in a glass case.
. . . Beside her, cross-legged on the floor, sat a
tall man of fifty or more, with a lined, black face
and a fringe of grizzled hair. . . . Long, long fingers, spread suddenly wide as he smiled at her
out of the dark forest.

"Hallo, Little Red Riding Hood."

But it was not simply an extraordinary room that I had
imagined. It was the whole essence of the world of *Wolf.* Everything important in the book is crystallized in that room and the
way Cassy experiences it: Her distrust of any but the most prosaic reality; her automatic search for limits and boundaries; her
identity as Little Red Riding Hood; even the feeling of danger
that surrounds her.

The curious thing is that, once the picture had formed, I
could see where it had sprung from. It owed a lot to *The Trials
and Tribulations of Little Red Riding Hood*, a book of variant versions which was lent to me by the children's editor at the
Oxford University Press. And to a squat I once visited in
Lewes, in Sussex. And to the room in which Oscar Wilde's
mother used to entertain her visitors, where the frames of the
huge mirrors were draped in cloth, to give an illusion of infinitely receding space. But I could never, consciously, have fit-
ted all those things together to make Goldie's mirror-room.
And I certainly could not have endowed the room with the terrifying, numinous significance that hit me as soon as Cassy
opened the door. But while I was concentrating on prosaic
details, like the decaying plaster of the hall, my unconscious
mind was constructing the world I wanted to enter.

That combination of vividly imagined details and disproportionate meaning is characteristic of the land at the top of the beanstalk. We experience the objects in it more acutely than we experience any objects in the real world, so that they take on the numinous significance of objects in a dream. And, like a dream, the imagined world contains the general within the particular. It is lit up by archetypal patterns, not *in spite* of its reality, but *because* of it.

Even in our waking life this happens. If we set ourselves truly to perceive a garden — or an island, or a street in the Gorbals — without preconceptions, and without intellectualizing what we see, we come to feel that the object in itself has some meaning that we cannot quite grasp.

Try standing quite still, underneath a large tree. With your hands on its trunk and your eyes looking up at the leaves. Listen to the branches rustling. Rub your fingers against the bark and sniff them. The more you try to concentrate on form and color and smell, the more you will begin to feel that the tree, in some mysterious way, relates to you. That its existence implies something about your own.

> One of the deepest and strangest of all human moods [says G. K. Chesterton] is the mood which will suddenly strike us perhaps in a garden at night, or deep in sloping meadows, the feeling that every flower and leaf has just uttered something stupendously direct and important, and that we have by a prodigy of imbecility not heard or understood it.

If this is so when we contemplate ordinary, unstructured reality, how much more does it seem so when we read a book. There, we know that the details have been selected by another human mind. Even if we are reading about material objects, neutrally reported, we know that someone has chosen those objects, out of everything there is or could be, not only in this world, but in every imaginable world.

Without that detailed, careful choice, that insistence on *this*, rather than *that*, there can be no imagined world.

Consider Jack again. Some people would argue that his story appeals to us because he defeats what we all fear, and gains what we all desire. Surely the giant is the ultimate enemy: an enemy too huge to be fought, who thunders relentlessly after Jack, planning to *eat him up.* And surely the treasure Jack steals represents the ultimate security: limitless wealth, which can solve all his worries.

People who argue like that would say that these generalities lie at the heart of *Jack and the Beanstalk.* That they are what it is about. But the *story* of Jack and the Beanstalk has nothing to do with general fears and desires. It is not *about* getting rid of want and overcoming physical danger—any more than it is *about* the dangers and rewards of leaving one's childhood home and earning one's own living. Or *about* Jack's coming to terms with the suddenly erect phallic beanstalk and killing the father figure at the top. All sorts of things can be grafted onto a good story, but if we think of the beanstalk as a phallic symbol, we have made the story less substantial, and not more meaningful. Jack is not just any boy. He is a particular lazy, incompetent boy. The treasure he steals is not just any treasure. It is (among other things) a golden harp with a human face, which shrieks *Master! Master!* when any stranger picks it up. And Jack's enemy is not just any giant. He is the giant who stalks round the kitchen sniffing. Saying:

> "Fee fi fo fum.
> I smell the blood of an Englishman.
> Be he live or be he dead,
> I'll grind his bones to make my bread."

It is by these details that we know we are in another world, and that can be proved by a simple test. If you want to make that world more real to yourself, it is no use asking what the giant symbolizes. You must ask yourself how he *smells*.

And only a children's book can tell you straight out. Pick up an adult novel which tells you how the giant smells, and (if it is a serious novel) you will be forced to ask yourself the purpose of the statement. Does his smell indicate something about his particular cultural pattern of eating and washing? Is it meant to tell us something about his social class? Or to indicate his role as a symbolic outcast from normal humanity? Or is it, perhaps, some kind of sexual signal, a gigantic pheromone, repellent to people, but absolutely irresistible to female giants? What does the smell *mean?*

Only a children's author is allowed to say: the giant smells like that because—that is what he *does* smell like. Indeed, as things are, it is only in children's books that a character can be a giant because he *is* a giant. Serious adult novels have fallen prey to the defensive objectivity which we are taught as a central part of our education. We are taught (and it is necessary) to look for the journalist behind every newspaper headline, and the biased mind behind every theory. It is we, the readers, who must be in control, not the author or (worse still) the story itself. Unless we pick up all the hints and clues and allusions that the author has built into his created world, we feel that we have not properly read a novel, and to do that we must remain detached and watchful. We must not lose touch with reality.

In that frame of mind, we shall never enter any world but our own. We shall simply perceive, from outside, the nature of those worlds apart. But children's books—because they are only for children—give us permission to take our feet from the ground. They transport us to idiosyncratic but consistent worlds that we can enter without looking over our shoulders to see whether we are being clever enough to catch the author's points.

Because children's writers have, generally speaking, no time for making clever points. Knowing that they have an inexperienced and partly ignorant audience, they cannot present a fictional world by allusion to the common world which we all share. They must start from scratch, concentrating on visualizing everything very clearly so that it can be properly communicated.

And, by virtue of that concentration, and that visualization, they conjure the thing they have despaired of creating.

Imagination is not a matter of cleverness, not a question of meticulous work or intellectual grasp. It demands involvement, and daring, and sheer effrontery. The actor John Malkovich was once given the part of a blind man. He described, afterward, how the film company had lent him a chauffeured car to take him to a home for blind people, so that he could observe them every day for a month. After the first day or so, he avoided the home and persuaded the chauffeur to take him to used car lots instead. When challenged, he said, "I needed to buy a car, and I was looking for a Studebaker." When challenged further, he said, "I can't work like that. It's not what I do. All that research is a failure of imagination, isn't it?" But he played his part so convincingly that visitors to the set of the film thought that he was, indeed, blind.

He was far from blind. He was obeying that precept which a painter once gave to a pupil as the only one truly necessary for creative imagination: *Never recognize. Always see.*

If you want a good view, you have to climb up high.

These remarks were made at *Worlds Apart*, CLNE at Oxford University, Oxford, England, in 1992.

LEAPING OFF THE PORCH

SHARON CREECH

One of my favorite beginnings is from Coleridge's unfinished poem, "Kubla Khan":

> In Xanadu did Kubla Khan
> A stately pleasure dome decree:
> Where Alph, the sacred river, ran
> Through caverns measureless to man
> Down to a sunless sea. . . .

Ah. The hypnotic sound of that opening. The pounding images: the stately dome, the sacred river, the measureless caverns, the sunless sea. I see the place in my mind. I am there, transported, already, five lines into the poem: twenty-six words.

I love the story behind the composition of this poem and the explanation for why it remains unfinished. I'm sure many of you know this explanation: that the fragment of "Kubla Khan" came to Coleridge in a drug-induced sleep, that the "images rose up before him as *things*," and that when he awoke he immediately began to record the images on paper. But! He was, so he claimed, unfortunately interrupted by a "person from Porlock," and on returning to his work, Coleridge found that the remaining images had dispersed—disappeared—to return nevermore.

Think of it: Interrupted! Gone! Unfinished! No ending!

I also love the twentieth-century poem by Stevie Smith, which reflects on this incident, this interruption of Coleridge's muse. In Smith's poem, "Thoughts about the Person from Porlock," the speaker suspects that Coleridge was already stuck, but blames his visitor. Unlike Coleridge, however, the speaker in Smith's poem is *hungry* for interruption, longing for a person from Porlock to bring her thoughts to an end.

There are times when I, like the speaker in Smith's poem, keep going to the window and gazing out, longing to be interrupted by a person from Porlock, but there are also times when I am so deep in my own measureless caverns that I wouldn't hear the person from Porlock if he battered down the door—or if I did hear him, he'd probably become a character in whatever I was working on at the time.

When I started writing, it wasn't a matter of either fearing or longing for interruptions. It was more a matter of how to begin. I'd like to back up to 1967 when I took my first writing course, at Hiram College. On the first day of class, the professor, a visiting British writer, announced our assignment for the semester: "Write a novel." He didn't say how one actually writes a novel, or what sort of novel we might attempt, just *write a novel.* We had one week to complete the first chapter.

I spent most of the next week in a sort of stupor, imitating the writers I'd seen in movies. You drink, right? You smoke, right? (Remember, this was 1967.) You rip pages out of the typewriter and toss them on the floor, and you run your hands through your hair. None of it helped. By the sixth day I was getting worried. No novel. No page one. No beginning. No *idea.*

(An aside: When someone once asked Albert Einstein if he kept a journal of ideas, he replied, "Well, I only ever had the *one* idea!")

So there I was, with no ideas, no knowledge of how to begin. I'd have to cheat: I'd tell something that really happened. And so I wrote about a trip that my boyfriend and I had taken the previous summer. In a beat-up Volkswagen, we had driven from Ohio to Mexico. I changed all the characters' names, of course, and because my memory is somewhat deficient, I had to invent a lot.

My author-professor had two comments on my novel-in-progress. The first was that I had chosen terrible names for my characters. *Boring,* he said. The second comment was this: "I like your beginning: 'Last summer we drove from Ohio to Mexico.' Perfect!" he said. "The classical, archetypal journey structure. Excellent!"

"Oh, yes," I said. "The journey structure. Hmmm." I, a senior English major, hadn't a clue as to what the classical, archetypal journey structure was. I don't think this was the fault of my professors. I probably hadn't been listening. And I didn't bother to find out then what that journey structure was; on I plunged with my journey from Ohio to Mexico, and although I didn't finish the novel, I had learned that a classical, archetypal journey structure (whatever that might be) was probably a good thing to use.

Later, in graduate school, I studied with more writers—some whizzing in and out for quick workshops, some pausing for a semester, such as John Gardner, James Dickey, John Irving, Marvin Bell, and Gordon Lish. One day John Gardner said: "Most stories rely on one of two classical and archetypal structures. . . ." I sat up. I heard those words *classical* and *archetypal.* Those two structures, he said, were *the stranger comes to town* and *the journey.* Ah!

I understood that the stranger—whether it was the ghost in *Hamlet* or Chillingworth in *The Scarlet Letter*—was also a metaphorical one, with potential to shape our lives, and the journey—whether it was the Joads' trek across America in *The Grapes of Wrath* or Odysseus's journey home to Ithaca—was also a metaphorical one, of the self for understanding. It all seemed to come down to our journeys and our strangers: where and how we go and who we meet, in the world and in our minds and in our hearts. There would be more, much more, for me to learn about archetypal journeys and strangers, but at that point I saw how these structures would offer me endless frames for endless stories.

What a frame offers is the skeleton for shape; it offers a beginning point and an ending, and it suggests the height and depth and width of the middle. You can begin with the arrival of the stranger, and you end with either the departure of the stranger or the aftereffects of his intrusion. You can begin with the first day of the journey and end with the last day of the journey. It's *okay* to do this. Even if lots and lots and lots of writers have done this, it is not only okay; it is *good*.

Surrounding the house in which I grew up, on Buxton Road in South Euclid, Ohio, was a small yard. Steps from the porch led down into the front yard, in which stood a fine maple tree. At the back of the house was another yard, bordered by my father's flower gardens on two sides and by his vegetable garden on the third side. A garage and driveway stood beside the house.

When I was nine, and ten, and probably when I was eleven, I did a lot of climbing and running. This was a route I often took, running, and starting from the porch: down the front steps, across the yard, up the maple tree, down the maple tree, between house and hedge, over low patio wall, down the back

yard, around the birdbath, back up alongside the vegetable garden, up the pear tree and onto the top of the garage, across the
garage and down the other side (a jump), along the driveway,
and back to the porch.

I'd time this route, counting. Round and round and round.
I always started from the porch, and ended up at the porch.
Round and round and round. Hundreds of times.

You might think this seems a bit dimwitted—this endless
repetition of the same route. But it *wasn't* the same route. Each
time there was something new to see, to notice. Maybe it was
six burgundy peonies on one round, a smooth white stone on
another round, a dead possum on the next round. The goal was
not only to run the lap faster each time, but also to find something new each time.

Each time I sit down to write, I have this feeling that I'm
circling back—moving round and round, returning to the place
and the feelings of a younger me, finding something new each
time, and emerging at the end of each day's writing, blinking at
the adult me, feeling a bit dizzy.

It wasn't until recently that I looked back at those structural
frames of my books—those stranger and journey structures—
and saw that the *shape* of each was circular. In some the circle is
chronological: the span of a day, or a week, or a season, with the
commencement of a new day/week/season implied at the end; in
some the circle is also geographical: from Bybanks to Ohio to
Idaho and back to Bybanks. These circles echo and enclose thematic cycles—birth to death to rebirth; beginnings to endings to
beginnings.

I realize that so far I have mentioned *structural frames* (the
journey and the stranger) and *shape* (a circular one, especially),
and even I am a bit confused: Are structure and shape different
entities? Well, today they are. I suppose I am using the *journey
structure* and the *stranger structure* to suggest the skeletal frame of

plot, and the *circular shape* to suggest a refinement of that structure. The journeys could be linear or triangular—or circular. The stranger visit could be played out linearly or triangularly— or circularly.

So I found circular journeys and circular stranger stories in my books. These were not consciously planned structures, shapes, or themes. They evolved as I was writing, and although I may have been able to say, near the end of a first draft, "Oh, look what we have here—a cycle," and "Ah, so I am really talking about that same old preoccupation of mine: life never-ending," I wasn't aware of these things in the blush of first writing, in that running, running stage where I am just leaping here, leaping there, following my characters as they run. I was not aware until the end that they'd run round and round, and ended up back on the front porch, ready to start again.

I suspect that the structure and shape are subconsciously chosen, and that either they echo the circular theme of which I am not yet conscious—or that they influence the theme. Does the form shape the content, or does the content shape the form? I don't have an answer for this, but I think, in my case, it is probably some of each. They are shaping each other.

When I begin a book I feel like that "smoothbeautiful horse" of e. e. cummings's poem "the little horse is newlY." I know nothing, but feel everything. All around me is perfectly a strangeness of light and smell, of a world that is welcoming me in, a world full of smoothbeautiful folds in which lies the breathing and silence of that someone—that character who is about to break her silence.

Walk Two Moons first began in the voice of Mary Lou Finney, recounting what-happened-after-she-turned-in-that-summer-journal of *Absolutely Normal Chaos*. The next drafts were in the voice of Phoebe Winterbottom, who leaped onto paper one day, and who took over with her lively imagination, her wild flights of fancy. And finally emerged the voice of Salamanca Tree Hiddle, a stubborn, ornery country girl at heart, who fishes in the air.

Salamanca was born out of one of my inspiration naps—I also call them research naps. They are not the drug-induced naps that Coleridge took, however. I usually work a long morning writing, and then when my brain becomes too muddled, I lie down on my bed, usually with another book, and I read until I doze off. When I awake about an hour later, the muddle has cleared, and something surfaces: often this is an image so clear—maybe as clear as Coleridge's Kubla Khan vision might have appeared to him.

One afternoon, some of the things in my muddled head, as I drifted off to sleep, were Mary Lou and Phoebe and my grown children, who were off in the U.S. at college. Also floating in there was a fortune cookie message I'd rediscovered in the bottom of my purse: "Don't judge a man until you've walked two moons in his moccasins."

I awoke an hour later to this line floating in my head: "Gramps says that I'm a country girl at heart, and that is true." It's the opening line of *Walk Two Moons*. . . .

Recently I read an article by the writer Lorrie Moore, who commented on stories that begin "up close, on the heart's porch." I love that image—up close, on the heart's *porch*! That is how I felt about that opening line right from the start—"Gramps says that I'm a country girl at heart, and that is true." It seemed to begin up so close to Salamanca, on her own heart's porch.

Salamanca, newlY born, leaped into the world, pulling with her Mary Lou and Phoebe and thoughts of separated parents and children and journeys and moccasins. About a third of the way through this new version I realized that what I had here was, what do you know, not only a *classical, archetypal stranger* story (with *lots* of strangers), but also a *classical, archetypal journey* structure! There was going to be a beginning, a middle, and an end, by which time "stuff" would have happened. Strangers would have come and gone; a journey would have begun and middled and ended. It was going to be *okay.*

I didn't know what was going to happen on this journey. I just knew that Salamanca was going to Idaho to see her mother, to try to bring her home. I didn't know whether her mother was alive or dead, nor that Salamanca was going with her grandparents. I was in my "newlY born" horse phase, knowing nothing, but feeling so much, so unarticulated *much*!

That first line influenced me enormously: "Gramps says that I am a country girl at heart, and that is true." Every day when I sat down to write, I returned to that line, as if returning to my own porch. It seemed the whole of the story was in that line, but I had to keep returning to it, leaping off from that point and running a new lap, in order to uncover what that story was. Bit by bit I learned these things: There was a sincerity in her tone, and an innocence. Her grandfather was important to her. The country was important to her. But it took me a long time to figure out why she had added that phrase, "and that is true." Gramps says that I'm a country girl at heart, and *that is true.* Was it just a throwaway phrase or was there more to it than that?

Eventually I realized that Salamanca uses that particular phrase—and shortly afterward confesses to being inclined to "fish in the air"—because she is trying to tell the reader that she has had difficulty in accepting some truths, and in distinguishing between truth and fishing in the air. And so to me, in that first line, was the key to what Salamanca is doing. She is retelling the story of the most difficult thing she has faced: the truth. And the only way she can retell it to you is to unfold it slowly, to unfold it gently, in the same way she had unfolded it for herself—in the context of, amid the layers of, all the other things going on in her life, past and present.

I can now see that taking Salamanca on a trip across the States was a way for me to return, at least in my mind, to my home country, which I was missing, and to thoughts of parents and children who, like me and my own children, were separated. Although Sal's separation from her mother is a more dire situation than mine was (after all, my children had gone to the States with my blessings), at the time I was writing this book, I felt everything Sal did: terrible loss and emptiness and a strong, strong desire to go find my grown children and bring them home! Fortunately for them, I wrote the book instead.

I know that some writers plan their books out carefully before they begin writing, and I admire that, and I recognize that those writers might find my approach rather haphazard. But if I were to plan it out ahead of time, I fear I would not have the enthusiasm to write the book. One thing that is so exciting for me about writing is that leap off the porch, eager to see what will happen, and then *whoosh*—watching it unfold. I like the delicious, wild, coltish run of that first draft. I like knowing nothing, but feeling everything. I like following the characters into regions I might have been reluctant to allow them to go if I'd already planned their journey.

I revise later. I reshape and cut and add and fix, and all of these revisions are more laps, during which I run the circuit again, looking for new things and clearing some of the clutter away.

The interior shape of *Walk Two Moons* follows the shape of a leisurely journey—the weaving in and out; a leisurely swim—stroking across the water and then diving down, down, down, and resurfacing, and diving again; or even, perhaps, the shape of running laps—returning with each segment to Gram and Gramps.

It wasn't until Salamanca and her grandparents were about to cross the Idaho state line that I saw what was to come. I'd picked up vibrations in my rereading—quivers of layers I hadn't seen before. Some of the vibrations were in the things Sal had told her friends, in the way she said them; some were inherent in that westward—toward sunset, if you will—journey (as opposed to eastward and sunrise); and some were in the grandparents, in the behavior, especially of Gram, from the start of the trip.

Gram seemed to be exhibiting symptoms of an impending stroke from the beginning; her memory lapses, her mood swings. And I saw her zest for each moment as a manifestation—perhaps—of a premonition that she was taking her last journey.

With Sal and her mother, what I saw was this: Sal is at an age where girls normally begin to separate from their mothers, but her normal weaning has been interrupted by her mother's sudden departure and continued absence. Sal's fishing in the air is a sign of her hopes, her wishes, her prayers that she will find her mother again, that she is not forever gone. The farther we went on that journey, Sal and I, the more it seemed that what Sal was really searching for was the "spirit" of her mother—perhaps what we all eventually seek from our parents.

The grave loomed up before me as we descended that mountain. I felt as if Sal and I were being swept down through "caverns measureless to man / Down to a sunless sea." We get to the grave, and what happens—to Sal, and to me? In one moment, we know that the mother—her body—is "dead," and in the next moment we see that the spirit of the mother is alive, absolutely and always and forever. Sal *does* bring her mother home with her. To paraphrase Mary Lou Finney: *Alpha and omega and alpha again. . . .*

I was aware in that grave scene that for a long, long time I had been trying to come to grips with people's absences: my father's death, my friend's death, my children's absence, all my family so far away over the ocean, even my students and friends departing so soon after I'd come to know them (this is a fact of life in international schools, but no less difficult for being a fact of life). And the way I had learned to deal with these absences was to surround myself with photos and to make these people very, very vivid in my mind—so vivid that what happened was this: Those who had died were as "alive" in my mind as those who were living an ocean away.

Odd. This was not fishing in the air; this was an emotional *truth*. Maybe I, like Sal, had found that gossamer line at which truth and "fishing in the air" merge.

I was, in that grave scene, comforted, as Sal is, to *really* know, to *really* feel the presence of a loved one, even in his or her physical absence. Sal senses that her mother is in the birds, the trees, in Bybanks, and in her, and that is how I feel about all the people I'm separated from: They are all around me, they are in me, and I hope I'm in them too.

I had earlier envisioned that the trip would end in Idaho, but when Salamanca got to Idaho, I saw all those cycles: of the tide rising and falling, rising and falling; and of the reincarnation myths Sal's mother has told her and to which she clings, myths with their images of birds and sky and trees. That's when I knew that Salamanca would return, full circle, to Bybanks. I see the ending, when Sal returns eastward to Bybanks, as another beginning for her, the beginning of this new self, aware of what is "true" but knowing that she will still, at times, "fish in the air," and knowing now *why* she fishes in the air.

To me, what happens in Idaho is the emotional ending of the book, but the literal ending is in those final two words: *huzza, huzza*. Salamanca is not yet able to say them with exclamation, like her grandmother, or like Mary Lou Finney could shout

"Alpha and Omega!" But in echoing her grandmother's phrase, Salamanca carries on all that she has learned from both mother and grandmother. And I knew that Sal would be okay—better than okay—if she could say *huzza, huzza.*

I'd like to back up now and talk about "inevitability" in endings. Most books on writing advise that endings should be—should appear—inevitable, and I was fortunate with *Walk Two Moons.* The ending did rise up, surprising me with its apparent inevitability. But it is not always so when I write. Often I agonize over endings. *Inevitable? Inevitable?* How can we possibly know what is *inevitable*? All we know is that "it" will end. But how it will end—ah, there's the rub.

There are days when I see a dozen possible endings simultaneously. Each could be possible, based on what has gone before. Isn't that the writer's job—to imagine the possibilities? I am usually reluctant to indulge in that final judgmental act of bringing my characters to their ends. I have no qualms about bringing them into their "perfectly strange" worlds, but to ease them out of their worlds—that's so very much harder, I think. To limit them to just one end? I want to give them *infinite* ends.

Often, my first-draft endings are rather grim. Like the stage at the end of a Shakespearean tragedy, my own stage is often littered with dead bodies. In the first draft of *Absolutely Normal Chaos,* for example, I killed off poor Carl Ray. But in the next run-through, I feel terribly guilty. I would like *my* Creator to deal more benevolently with *me,* after all. I want to come back as Estsanatlehi, that Navajo woman Salamanca mentions, the one who grows from baby to mother to old woman, and then turns into a baby again, and on and on she goes, living a thousand, thousand lives. So in the next draft, I usually resurrect everyone and bring in the sun. Carl Ray was resurrected, and so was Gram, in these sunny run-throughs.

After many more rounds, the final endings are usually somewhere in between. There *is* death, because I am preoccupied with losing people, but there is also resurrection—of spirit—and someone carries on, someone has hope.

I suppose that my inclination to repeat that cyclical shape says something about my inner workings, my view of the world, that I do see life as cyclical, or, more accurately, I yearn for it to be so. A cycle implies a continuum, it implies life never-ending, it implies immortality.

Speaking of immortality, I have another aside for you: When someone from my publisher phoned shortly after the announcement was made that *Walk Two Moons* had received the Newbery Medal, I said, "What does this mean—exactly?"

She said, "It means—it means—*immortality*!"

Oh. *Immortality.* I was reminded of something Woody Allen once said. He said, "I don't want to achieve immortality through my work; I want to achieve it through *not dying.*"

I have a few small stories to tell you yet. I'm moving back to the porch, and I'm going to run three laps. They're about journeys and strangers and circles; the power of memory and imagination; and endings and beginnings.

Here's the first lap. 1958. I was thirteen years old. My family was vacationing at a Wisconsin lake, and one day we went for a drive: my parents, my three brothers, my sister, and I. My father said that we were going to a small town up north, and when we reached it, he said, "I was born here. Somewhere along here—I'll recognize the place—" and he scanned the fields and the crossroads as we crept along.

"What? Born *here*?" It seemed a mighty revelation, a secret just revealed. We, too, scanned the fields.

He described the house: a farmhouse, small and gray; and he described the green fields that spread out around it, and the clear river that ran nearby, in which he had learned to fish.

We drove and drove. We circled back. Finally, my father pulled up beside a field we had passed several times already. He got out of the car and waded through the grass. We followed him, running alongside. He crossed this field, stepped through a rim of trees at the far end, and there, beyond the trees, was a river. Then he returned to the field and said, "This is it. This is where I was born."

"Here?" we said. "In the *field*?"

"No," he said. "In a house—a small, gray house—"

"But where is the house?" we demanded.

"It's gone," he said.

And we all piled back in the car, and drove in silence to the lake, and there I followed my father, joining him in the rowboat. He rowed steadily out to the middle of the lake, dropped the anchor, and passed me a fishing rod and a can of worms. We baited our hooks and cast our lines.

And inside I was filled with such disappointment, such longing. Why couldn't the house have been there? Why couldn't it have waited for him?

But as I stared at the water, I formed an image of that house, piece by piece—I must have wanted to see it *so* badly! Glimpses of it floated up from the depths of the lake, glimpses of the roof, the walls, the windows, until I saw, distinctly, that small gray house, with fields around it and the river behind. I saw a boy coming out of the house, carrying a fishing pole, and running across the field and through the trees to the edge of the river, where he cast his line into the water.

There it all was: the house, the boy, the fields, as if, together, we had raised them from the water. And when I saw this image, I turned to my father, hardly able to contain myself. Had he seen it too? But his eyes were fixed on the water and he said not a word.

I tell you this story because it illustrates something about ourselves as strangers on our own journeys, and about the power of memory and imagination to fulfill a need and a longing to continue the circle. . . .

Here's the second lap. A few years ago, I was with my mother in Portsmouth, Ohio, the town in which she and my father met. We drove in search of the gas station where my father had worked at the time. We found the corner where it had stood, but the corner was empty now. My mother had that look on her face, the same one my father had when he couldn't find his small gray house.

"But it was there," my mother said at last. "It was 1940. The pumps were there—the building was there—I was walking along—see there? He called to me. He offered me a Coca-Cola—"

I could see it in my mind. I could see it clearly. And I would have sat there much longer, imagining it, but my mother said, "Let's go. It's gone."

No! I wanted to say. *No, it is not gone.* I did not want her "it's gone" to be the Porlockian who interrupts the scene. That scene was still vivid in her mind, just as my father's small gray house was vivid in his mind, so vivid that they had been able to transplant these scenes into my mind, into me—and my urge, it is so strong, is to transfer them to you.

Here is lap number three. My mother's scene reminds me, eerily, of another one—my own. It was 1979. I had just arrived in England. It was a hot August evening. There was a thatched cottage and a courtyard and a stranger—there—and I was walking along near the roses—see there? The stranger called to me. He offered me some ice cubes.

I *married* him.

Journeys and strangers. Memory and imagination. Parents and children. Past and present. Beginnings and endings. It's all squished in there together, isn't it?

Stories—their appeal is so strong to us, and why is this? I think it is partly because, whether as reader or writer, we see each story as an invitation: Come along, walk with us a while, come on our journeys. We can be Estsanatlehi. We can run a thousand, thousand laps. We can live a thousand, thousand lives. With each story, we will be born into a perfectly strange world, knowing nothing but feeling everything, and we will encounter a welcoming dream, and at the end of each story there is the satisfaction of having completed our journey, enriched by having lived that life and meeting those strangers, but also resurrected—knowing that we can live it, and many other lives, all over again.

Huzza, huzza and *Alpha and Omega*!

Portions of "Leaping off the Porch" previously appeared in *Fishing in the Air: A Writer's Journeys*, published by the Friends of  the CCBC, Inc., Madison, Wisconsin, 1996. These remarks were made at *Endings and Beginnings: The Shape of Story*, CLNE at Harvard University, Cambridge, Massachusetts, in 1996.

JACK AND GUY AND ROSIE

MAURICE SENDAK

The creative process is a rambling business, so I will tell you in a rambling way the genesis of *We Are All in the Dumps with Jack and Guy*.

In 1963 I had just finished *Where the Wild Things Are*. When it was published, it received many hard knocks from critics, and it was considered fearful and ugly and inappropriate, which to the thirty-three-year-old artist was very discouraging. So I went back to nursery rhymes.

I've always been in love with nursery rhymes, and I decided to do a series of books. In fact, I was going to illustrate my own collection of the Mother Goose rhymes. It was a major project that was never accomplished, but I pulled together a whole series of nursery rhymes that I particularly loved and was preparing to illustrate them. But instead they fell out into various other books. *Higglety Pigglety Pop!* has a nursery rhyme. *In the Night Kitchen* has another. Every book I did thereafter has filched the nursery rhymes from the book that I never did.

I fell in love with the two verses "We're All in the Dumps" and "Jack and Guy." They're in the Oxford University collection of Mother Goose by Peter and Iona Opie. Some verses have bits of history attached to them, but these have none. That's how I got to know the Opies, because I wrote them a letter and asked whether they could tell me anything about these particular rhymes, and they could not. But they shared my enthusiasm for these strange little pieces.

In 1964 or 1965 I did my version of *We Are All in the Dumps with Jack and Guy*. I did a dummy, wrote a book with many, many colored pictures, finished it, and showed it to my editor at Harper's, Ursula Nordstrom. She hated it. She thought the rhymes made no sense, but she didn't mind the rhymes not making sense. She just didn't think I had made any sense of the rhymes, that I hadn't given them any particular life. So, after being crabby for a few months, I gave it up. I still have that version of the book. It's a very sixties book, very psychobabble. It's very laid back, very flower child. It's very foolishly optimistic. In other words, it's very bad. And apparently I forgot about it because I went on to do many other works, and even left the profession of children's books when I turned fifty to go into stage design for opera, which had been my first love.

In 1991 or 1992, I was doing a Mozart opera. We were in rehearsal in Los Angeles, and anybody who knows Los Angeles knows you don't walk in the city of Los Angeles. We were in rehearsal late at the opera house, and then we were driven back to our hotels. On the way back to the hotel, past midnight, we passed Rodeo Drive, which is the most incredibly expensive street in the cosmos. It's a freak street, and I hadn't seen this, so I was curious to look at it.

It was very well lit, but to my astonishment in the middle of the street was a cardboard box, a food box from a grocery store. There's a pair of naked black feet, a child's feet, sticking out of the box. So obviously a kid was sleeping in a cardboard box on Rodeo Drive, and the juxtaposition was amazing.

On the way back to the hotel, the whole verse came into my
head. It's probably the first time I had thought of it in more than
twenty years, and I realized that "We are all in the dumps" back
in the sixties had meant depression, because in the sixties you
were no one if you were not seeing a psychiatrist. So the word
"dumps" meant sad or depressed, and suddenly, I realized in the
nineties "dumps" literally means dumps, garbage, junk, and also
people treated in that manner.

So the line and the verse suddenly had a new kind of significance.

I keep a journal on work trips, and I was trying to remember the verse, but I could only remember the first line. And I
kept thinking of that kid sleeping on Rodeo Drive. And the
whole idea of the book hadn't left my head at all. The nervous
system in the brain of us weird people called creative artists
constantly functions without our knowledge. Obviously, this
tiresome creative process had been mulling this verse over for
many years, for over two decades.

The verses go:

> We are all the dumps
> For diamonds are trumps.
> The kittens are gone to Saint Paul's.
> The baby is bit,
> The moon's in a fit,
> And the houses are built without walls.

That's the first one. The second one:

> Jack and Guy went up in the sky
> And they found a little boy with one black eye.
> Come, says Jack, let's knock him on the head.
> No, says Guy, let's buy him some bread.

You buy one loaf and I'll buy two
And we'll raise him up as other folk do.

Now these two verses have nothing to do with each other whatsoever, except in my feverish mind. I clung to the idea that they had to go together in some way, which I had failed to achieve in 1964.

Now I was reenergized. Could I bring them together? I thought that kid whose face I never saw and never will see would be the hero of my book. Jack and Guy would be two little toughs, like out of Charles Dickens or maybe out of movies I saw when I was a kid, maybe Pat O'Brien and James Cagney, or two boys from *Oliver Twist* who worked for Fagan and stole things in the streets. They would be these two roughneck kids who live in the dumps.

That's the beginning of the book right there. Then I have Jack and Guy for one verse now living in dumpsville from the other verse.

Then you've got to solve very peculiar, obscure lines like "diamonds are trumps." What the hell does that mean? The fun was making it mean something, and making it mean ultimately in its subtext what all my books have always meant to me, which is: How do children survive under the best conditions with loving parents, or worse, with unloving parents—how do kids make out? That was the theme of *Wild Things*—Max has a perfectly happy, secure home, but he has a temper tantrum. On normal days, his mother smiles and tolerates it. But he picks the wrong day. She gets mad, and to his astonishment, she has a temper as violent as his. Even worse, she has more power than he does. She can deprive him of food and of freedom. So he goes into a fantasy. That's how he makes out. He goes into a fantasy and gets his revenge on wild things through his imagination. In the end, he discovers that in spite of the argument, she had it worse. She feeds him. Life goes on. It probably will go on this way until he's thirty-five and moves out.

Then, every book after that had to do with kids and what kids do to survive. In certain very brief moments that go by in seconds, how do they solve problems when they have no experience and no logic and they don't get any help? And they have to survive. We all did it. Everybody in this room had those moments when we had to figure out what to do by ourselves. My favorite moment in one of my books is in *Outside Over There*, when a little girl has to determine what to do when her father's away at sea, when her mother is lost in abstraction because she misses the father, and when she, only a mere nine-year-old, is dumped with the responsibility of a baby, whom she loves and detests, all at the same time. I know that from experience because my sister was stuck with me, and I remember the days she loved me, and I hid on the days that she hated me; but that, too, is the fate of all of us human animals who happen to be siblings.

We Are All in the Dumps with Jack and Guy is all about kids *in extremis*. Max had parents. Ida had parents. Mickey had parents, though he didn't see them, but in fact all the children of my books in the sixties, seventies, and eighties were good, healthy, middle-class kids. Whatever their problems, they were loved by the end of the book and reunited with the family.

Dumps is the first book that says there are kids out there who have no families, are reunited with nobody who is an adult. There's no one to take care of them, and life is rough.

I wanted to do a book about them, and how the human animal, even one the size of a child, must make a family, must survive, must be loved, must be cared for, must grow up. That's what these kids do. They just make a family. Jack and Guy adopt a little lost baby, and they live in the dumps and come hell or high water, they're going to make it. If I didn't believe they were going to make it, I'd be in a lot of trouble.

I'm sure most of you have read the Carnegie Report that came out a month or two ago, about the millions of children in this country who will never learn to read or write or be normal, healthy human beings because they're abused, bashed about. It's like the kids in *Dumps,* and we're going to have to contend with these kids when they grow up. And nobody's really doing anything about it yet.

So in our little, humble, simple ways, in publishing and otherwise, I think we almost become soldiers in a new war, which is to take on the salvation of the children. That sounds grandiose, but it's how I felt when I did this book.

On a few of the motifs: For one thing, I'm moon crazy. You'll find a moon in every book I've ever done, and I know that since childhood I have had a weird fascination with the moon. I remember, as a very small child, staring and staring and staring. So to me, it's perfectly natural that the moon appears in all my books, but the moon in this book is particular, and there is one picture during a card-playing scene where the moon appears three times: Someone asked me what was the logic of the moon appearing three times. You ask about logic in this book?—forget it!—but there was logic for me: The moon is looking with great anxiety on what's happening on earth. She is very concerned about the children. She's watching the card game, *boom boom boom,* and it was my mother.

Now if you, like me, like the child who was Rosie in *Really Rosie,* were an urban child, you were not allowed to go into the street by yourself. You were warned: *If you go into the street!* You cannot cross the street or you will get killed. Your mother knew best, so you wouldn't step a toe into the street because you would be run over. The toe would be run over, and then the rest of you wouldn't worry about entering the street. But sometimes you could not resist.

I found it most amazing in my mother that even when she

was lying in a near coma with a migraine headache, she would know when I was planning to cross the street. I would put out a foot, and her head would appear. "You'll get killed." Then it seemed her head would dart out of every window, and so what I did with the moon was illustrate my mother's head appearing three times anxiously, watching out for me and my brother and my sister. So the moon is my mother. It is my very worried mother who is watching. Moon mother.

As for Rosie? Rosie the child?—yes. This was 1941 and 1942, just starting the war. Every adult male except my father was in the army, and this was a very bad time. I was living in Brooklyn, and I took it upon myself this one summer to explore that for one of my projects. Even then I always gave myself projects, and my project was Rosie.

She was a kid who lived across the street. She was Sicilian. I observed her. She was amusing; she was charming. She was about nine, and I decided I would take down everything I could about this kid. I think, in retrospect, it was really to take my mind off the war, but it was a good project.

I'd sit by my window. I sat— it was a two-story house—and I'd look out on the streets. She was quite close, and I'd copy everything she said. I would draw her. Every day I'd spend two hours with Rosie. This was just over one summer. I filled about forty sketch books of Rosie, about twenty of which still exist. (I used to give them away to friends.) Why was I so fascinated? I didn't know then, but of course she was the archetypal kid for me: a tough child who endures everything. She was probably abused, in the language of the nineties, but in those days I didn't notice that.

One sensed something. One could hear the indifference in the voice of her mother when she called her. She had a little brother whose name, believe it or not, was Pudgy, and he was. She had to take care of him. She dressed up in her mother's clothes, as little girls do, but she was Maria Callas compared to most little girls. She was enormously gifted, even when she was a very small child.

She was wonderful. She made up movies that she never saw. She made up stories about her family that were not true but that were so beautifully convincing, they might as well have been true. She described the death of her grandmother. I was leaning out the window with my tongue hanging out in the street, because her *grandmother was alive*. In other words, she was an artist.

We never talked, because fourteen-year-olds don't talk to nine-year-olds, and nine-year-olds don't talk to fourteen-year-olds. But I remember the only time we almost talked was once when she was playing in the street. She was all dressed up, and her cousin came to live on the street, which was bad. Her name was Helen, and Helen was a very pragmatic, ordinary girl, and she was standing with Rosie in the middle of the street, and she looked up and our eyes locked, and Helen stared and she said loudly, "Why's that guy watching us? What's he doing?"

Rosie didn't turn around, and she had never shown me any evidence that she had seen me, but she said, as though it was a prepared answer, "His name is Johnson and he's taking my life down." She didn't know about Boswell. She didn't mean that. It was just a make-believe name. I was so impressed that she had taken me in and had ignored me all at the same time.

So all those notebooks became *The Sign on Rosie's Door*, in 1962 I think, and then *Really Rosie* with Carole King in 1972 — endless *Really Rosies*.

The only time we actually almost met was when I was interviewed on *20/20* or *60 Minutes* or one of those, many years ago. I went back to Brooklyn. They interviewed me on the street, and Brooklyn was insane. I was across the street from Rosie's house, and by this time, I was in my middle to late forties, and, of course, the only person in Brooklyn the inhabitants on the street were interested in was the guy who was interviewing me, because they recognized him. So of course I hated him. They were rushing up to him and saying, "Are you Joe Brown? Are you Joe Brown?" There were all these people clustered in Rosie's house, and I just couldn't resist, so before we put the cameras away, I said, "I may never come back here again, so I just want to go across the street." So the camera's following me, and I knocked on the door, and the door flew open, and the person who answered said, "Is that Joe Brown? Is that Joe Brown?"

"Yes, that's Joe Brown," I said. "I have just a very simple question, and you probably can't answer it, but I lived here when I was a little boy, and in this house there was a little girl, and I just wondered if you had any idea what happened to her. Her name was Rosie, and I can't remember her last name." "Oh, Rosie is my cousin." I said, "Wait—wait—I'm too excited." I said, "It can't be the same person." Well, she had lived there for many years, and they invited us in. It was a very Catholic home with crucifixes and saints along the walls, which I remembered glimpsing through the windows when I walked past to my house.

Now the guy who was holding the camera was extremely bored. Who is this kiddy book artist that they're interviewing? These dull little stories, he wanted to be with Madonna or somebody across town, and he comes in, he's chewing gum, and he's sort of dealing with it in this bored way. I said, "Please, I never remembered Rosie's last name." It was a very difficult Sicilian name, and even now I can't say it properly, but it was something like Timtumpuento. So this woman said, "Rosie Timtumpuento," and I said, "That's it!" and the man with the camera said, "Rosie Timtumpuento? You mean you've been talking about *her* all day?"

I looked at him and said yes.

"You've been talking about Rosie *Timtumpuento*?"

And I'm thinking, Why is he so impressed with her and not impressed with me?

He said, "Do you know—," and he had to sit down, and he broke out in a sweat, and they ran for a glass of water.

I said, "What is the matter with you?"

"I was engaged to her."

He knew this girl, which was just like a bad movie, and of course, he looked at us, and we didn't believe a word he said.

He said, "I want a phone. I want a phone." He phones his wife Rhoda because he lives nearby. "Rhoda, bring my yearbook."

The woman drives up. The door opens. She holds out a yearbook, and we grab it, sit down, turn the pages quickly. *Rosie Timtumpuento, with love to Brian*, whatever his name was.

It was she, and this is the first time I've seen her. This was her high school graduation picture, and she had been engaged to this jerk. Happily, she married someone else.

They're all getting cozy and drinking coffee and serving Jell-O, and they insist on my calling Rosie because she lives only seven blocks away. Sicilian families are like Jewish families. When you marry, you don't move more than five to seven blocks away from your parents, and there she was, and so we called, and they were speaking, and they put me on the phone, and she knew nothing of *The Sign on Rosie's Door* or *Really Rosie*.

This was some years ago. She was probably about forty or so. She had a lovely sweet voice, and I could hear her embarrassment. One of her kids was on the extension. She had three children, and the kid was very rough. He said, "What'd ya do?" Of course I really wanted to be speaking to his mother, and I was desperate. I said, *"Nutshell Library."* Finally, luck was on my side. I said, *"Wild Things."* "Hey, Ma, he did *Wild Things*!" So it was okay for me to talk to his mother.

We spoke. She invited me to Thanksgiving. I put together a

care package: *The Sign on Rosie's Door*, the record, the parapher-
nalia, all of the shebang, and I sent it off to her.

Then I had only one other phone conversation with her,
when she called me to thank me. She said she cried when she
read the book because she had no idea that anybody knew her
magic name was Melinda. She had no idea that anybody knew
her favorite song was "The Sunny Side of the Street." That I
could have been observing her without her knowing it.

I said, very attentively, "Did you ever, ever want to go and
be an actress or a singer or anything?"

She said, "Oh, yes, very much, but then I met my husband.
I fell in love, and after high school, I got married." Just the typical story, and she had three or four children. And he is a very
nice man. I spoke with him, too. He's a carpenter.

But everything that was incredible and vital and wonderful
about Rosie was gone.

Well, maybe it was still there, and she sounded like a marvelous person, and from the photograph she was a very beautiful young woman. But that particular arbitrary moment that I
chose to spend looking at her—that summer—was when I saw
something extraordinary, particularly cultivated in children and
especially in girl children. I mean, what were her options? Get
married. How could she go into show business, really?

It's not a sad story, particularly—but in some ways it is. And
then there is a sad note to this story, which is that her husband
called me, the third and last phone call I ever had from them, to
disinvite me to Thanksgiving. He was embarrassed, but the reason he did it, he explained, was that their first child had been
born with a serious disorder. Of course Rosie had fretted and
fretted. The child had died when he was ten years old and then
she apparently had severe depressions and mental breakdowns.
The orthodoxy of her treatment was that she not be overly
excited. He felt that this whole thing was too much: the radio,

who I was, *20/20*. He couldn't afford to risk it. So he begged my understanding, and he would explain it to her.

And that was it.

But to go back to the beginning: *We Are All in the Dumps with Jack and Guy*. There have been a lot of letters from grown-ups and children. Some grown-up letters were mean and angry, because they thought this subject wasn't suitable for children. More happily received were the letters from parents and teachers who were grateful that I had opened up that can of worms. This was a subject missing from the curriculum, and children *did* want to talk about these matters. But the best letters were the ones from children.

There was a teacher in Chicago who was a great fan of mine, but she was put off by the book. She admired it, but she couldn't imagine that this was for children. Since she trusted me, she wanted to chance it. She read it to her class of emotionally disturbed children in a suburb of Chicago. Then she wrote an article about it, which is how I got to hear the story. She had read the book (along with my other books), then she asked the class what it meant.

There were lots of marvelous answers, but I'll give you only two. One answer was from a little boy, who said the book's message was that you should eat a lot because all my books feed you: because in *Wild Things* there was dinner, and in *In the Night Kitchen* there was cake, and in *Higglety Pigglety Pop!* there was everything to eat. In *Jack and Guy* there was a lot of fresh bread. So he saw my works as a meal, which is as good a compliment as one could have.

The other comment was from a little girl, who said that the book means that the moon is everybody's mother. Which is the most profound thing anybody has said about that book. She really picked on something nobody has picked on, because there is basically no mother in the book. There's no female except some of the helpless little girls. The fact that she knew the moon was a mother I can't figure out, but what she did see happen was that the moon transformed herself into a mother cat, who takes care of her kittens, and then acts as a vehicle by which the children go back to where they came from. Obviously, she thought that's what a mother is supposed to do.

These remarks were made at *Image and Word: Patterns of Creativity*, CLNE at Mount Holyoke College, South Hadley, Massachusetts, in 1994.

PLAY'S THE THING

SARAH ELLIS

Play is one of the two universal childhood creative acts, the other being dreaming. I think it unlikely that among people who read and write there will be many who have forgotten about play. But, nonetheless, what with getting and spending and talking on cell phones, we can as adults find ourselves rather far removed from play. So I would like to invite you to join me, just for a few minutes, to listen in on two children playing.

The setting is a living room. It is February. It is after school. Lisbeth, eight, and Catherine, five, are playing with their dolls. I am sitting in an armchair, sort of reading a murder mystery but mostly listening in. The cast today consists of five dolls: three Barbies, one Skipper, and one large baby doll. The three Barbies are called Lucy, Mrs. Darling, and Bridget. The Skipper doll is called Sarah, and the baby doll is called Talking Doll. The Barbies are more or less normal, except that Bridget is missing one foot and has a head that falls off. Sarah, encased in spandex, is the only doll with any clothes on. In case of confusion, by the way, whenever the doll Sarah is around, I, the human Sarah, am referred to as Sarah-who-walks. Talking Doll is completely out of scale with the others. She used to talk when you pushed a button in her back, but Catherine drowned her in the wading pool the previous summer when she was playing Titanic, and now Talking Doll does not talk, except, of course, in the proper doll way.

The action on this day takes place on three levels: the floor, which is an aerobics center laid out with a piece of string in a circle, the coffee table, which is home with a bona fide Barbie bed and a tent made out of an opened paperback book, and the window seat, which is the lab and has a lot of half-constructed Tinker-toy stuff on it. The theme of the day seems to be keeping Barbie out of the lab.

As far as I can remember, the dialogue went something like this:

Lisbeth (holding Lucy): You can't come in the lab, said Lucy.

Catherine (making Bridget jump up and down in the air): But I want to.

Lisbeth: You're not allowed to. You'll just mess things up, said Lucy.

Catherine (shaking Bridget more vigorously): I won't mess things up. (Bridget's head flies off.)

Lisbeth: (picking up Mrs. Darling): Put on your head and go shopping, said Mrs. Darling.

Catherine, resignedly (while retrieving Bridget's head and recapitating her): Oh, all right.

This particular round of play went on from about half past three to five o'clock. As I tuned in and out of it, it seemed to me that very little else was happening in the way of plot. Sarah put on and took off her spandex a few times. The lab got a bit rearranged. People went to bed and got up, but mostly the hour and a half was spent scapegoating Bridget.

I think this was pretty typical. Apart from Lisbeth's eccentricity of saying "said so-and-so" after her lines, which I've never heard another child do, I think this scene of play was fairly unremarkable. But it was, to me, thinking as I was about creativity, fascinating.

The first thing I noticed was the ease with which the girls slid into the fantasy world. They didn't seem to decide to play. They just stepped in. There was no resistance to the fantasy world, and reality and fantasy were completely clearly defined. Once in, they played with absorption and intensity, with a kind of detachment from what was going on outside their corner of the room. In fact they almost seemed to be in a kind of meditative state. Their mother's mild suggestions about piano practice and hanging up coats were floating to them as from another universe. They were also able completely to remove themselves from any sense of purpose. Their play was all process and no product.

It was also anarchistic. It subverted adult expectations. When the girls received the Barbie dolls in a hand-me-down package from a cousin, their mother wasn't pleased. But she needn't have worried. These Barbies have little to do with teenage life. They aren't very interested in clothes, nudity being the style of the hour; they don't date or comb their hair. Likewise the Tinker toys aren't made into the clever windmill as pictured on the box lid, but into something far more surreal. Talking Doll doesn't say the things she is programmed to anymore. And, while Lisbeth and Catherine are rather kind and thoughtful, their dolls are not. Bridget, the disabled doll as it were, is the object of ostracism and vilification.

The raw material of Lisbeth's and Catherine's play could be characterized as life, stuff, and literature. *Life* plays a rather minor role. From the biochemist next door they borrowed the idea of a lab. From me they borrowed a name. And Bridget's low status might have had some origins in Lisbeth's not having the most enjoyable year in school. The *stuff* is all around them in their messy house. Most important, each new book they read or hear is promptly incorporated into their play. First and foremost are the Narnia characters, of whom the most long-lived seems to be Lucy.

And then Peter Pan, a more recent offering. Again, the surviving character here seems to be Mrs. Darling. (Odd, that; not the most compelling character, one would think.)

Finally, one thing that I noticed as dinner approached was that the pace of this play was very slow. Lots of repetition, lots of digression, long discussions of minute rule changes, lots of plain silence. The other raw material of play is *time*. The girls would occasionally emerge from their world for a bit and ask me to join in. But I couldn't gear down to the pace. I felt a bit like the mother in *A Stitch in Time* who rather desperately suggests a nice board game. Play really is the province of children.

And play really is like writing. Lisbeth and Catherine were making up plots and characters and conflict and dialogue and settings. Their mood and tone was like mine when I'm writing, where I float away from the world and time disappears, where at its best I get to make up my own rules, where I don't think about product but sink into the process, where I get to subvert my own adult expectations and actually escape from self.

The big difference between me writing and the girls playing was the sense of ease with which they entered their world. Would that I could enter so swiftly and stay there so effortlessly. Would that I could live so comfortably in two worlds simultaneously. Many authors have spoken of the oh-so-rare times when the work comes easily, and called these moments gifts. The playing child has these gifts in abundance. In this sense every child is gifted.

Loren Eiseley, in an essay called "The Mind as Nature," describes his own childhood, of living in two worlds as he played. "One was dark, hidden and self-examining, though in its own way not without compensations. The other world in which I somehow managed to exist was external, boisterous and what I suppose the average parent would call normal or extroverted. . . . I was living, you see, in a primitive world at the same time I was inhabiting the modern world. . . . Two worlds existed in which a boy, still a single unsplit personality, walked readily from one world to another, by day and by night, without anyone observing the individual boundaries he passed."

If what Lisbeth and Catherine were doing seemed like writing, in other ways it seemed much more like reading. Again, that sense of ease, the way it all seemed to pre-exist. William Gass in "Fiction and the Figures of Life" has a wonderful description of reading. "How easy it is to enter. An open book, an open eye, and the first page lifts like fragrance toward us as we read." I wonder if play is like some magical combination of writing and reading.

There is a kind of narrative satisfaction when playing children in books become writers. But I have a special fondness for those who don't, who just keep on as children who play. All children who play are genii. They create, sustain, and protect. *Genii* is the plural not only of *genie* but of *genius*, but it is only relatively late in the history of the word *genius* that it came to have its modern connotation of special gift. For hundreds of years it just meant sustaining spirit, a spirit contained in all things.

It is this all-encompassing definition that is to the point in children's play. The immense creativity that is demonstrated is not the province of the specially talented, the geniuses. Any child, given time, stuff, and literature, becomes a genius. Everyone who draws a face on a bean, or makes soldiers march across a carpet, or talks in funny voices, or decapitates a doll, or makes a sugar jar converse, is a genius. So is anyone who tells a story. So is anyone who reads one.

These remarks were made at *Image and Word: Patterns of Creativity*, CLNE at Mount Holyoke College, South Hadley, Massachusetts, in 1994.

WHEN WOLVES SING MOZART

GREGORY MAGUIRE

Not long ago, I arrived at an elementary school to spend some time with fourth- and fifth-grade writers. Alas, there'd been some sort of crisis in the kindergartens that morning—bursting water mains or escaped gerbils or something—and the principal asked me: Would I mind stopping off at the library on my way upstairs and talking to the kindergartners for fifteen or twenty minutes? "Tell them about the average day in the life of a writer," she said grimly. "Maybe that'll hold them."

I wasn't entirely sure.

However, I made my way to the library, where about forty little kids malingered in various stages of hysterical homesickness for their classroom. The librarian and teachers calmed the little ones down, and said, "Now this nice man is going to talk to us about being a writer. Can anyone tell me what a writer is?"

Well, no one could, not that day anyway. Lower lips wobbled dangerously. Since it seemed to me that telling them the story of an average day in my life would provoke tedium and amnesia at best, and maybe turn some of them off the alphabet for good, I decided my charge would be exercised well enough if I told them about one specific day instead of about a proto-typical day. "Do you want to know where I went last week?" I asked them. Enough kids nodded politely for me to take this as a mandate to continue.

"First I got in my car," I said, "then I turned the keys and the car went BROOOM BROOM, because it needs a tune-up. Then I got on the highway and headed toward the mountains in upstate New York." I won't take up twenty minutes telling you everything I told the kids, but I did make interesting sound effects to show them how the bad right rear tire went PUP-PUP-PUP- and then PUPUPUPUPUPUP and then PDDDDRRRR and then blew out, leaving me without a spare on the side of the Mass Pike. My car at the time was old and couldn't lock, and this being before the days I had converted to a computer, I was carrying with me my $950 secondhand-but-trusty-IBM Selectric II typewriter. I had to thumb a ride to the next tollbooth to call for help. When a truck slowed down and pulled off the road ahead, I ran up to it, and I told the driver I couldn't leave my valuables in my unlocked car at the side of the road. Then I ran back and collected my typewriter, as he waited, and I hoisted the heavy thing onto the seat beside me.

The truck driver looked a bit alarmed. "Why do you carry that thing around with you?" he asked. "I'm a writer, you never know when you might need to write something," I answered, perhaps a bit flippantly because I was so relieved to get a ride. "For instance," I added, "I probably should write you a thank-you letter for bringing me to the tollbooth."

Well, that was the end of *that* conversation. But there were other interesting people and exchanges to tell the kids about, as I got my tire replaced and jumped back into the car and at last made it, hours later than planned, to the mountainside chalet I had rented for the week in Indian Lake. I carted my luggage and typewriter into the house, and then strode out onto the deck. Across the deep, sweetly scented valley, a range of pine-forested mountains disappeared in hazy outlines. As it began to descend, the sun made the mountains turn pinkish. Back and forth on the deck, chipmunks skittered, looking like rolled-up pairs of socks sent bowling along. I was so happy, I told the kindergartners, so relieved to be there at last, that I opened up my mouth and sang at the hills the opening melodic line of Mozart's *Eine Kleine Nachtmusik,* that famous broken tonic chord: "*La,* la *la,* la *la* la la la laaaa. . . ."

Now there were some wolves who lived in the hills across the valley. They heard me singing. They threw their heads in the air and howled back the second line: "*Rrr,* rrr *rrr,* rrr *rrr* rrr rrr rrr rrrrrrr. . . ."

And we kept up an antiphonal chorus, for as much of the *Nachtmusik* as we could all remember. Then I went in and opened up my sleeping bag and lay down and drifted off to sleep. And that was one day in the life of a writer, I told the kids.

Now, writers pay attention to the world, I said; all artists do. Being an artist means looking, and seeing, first and foremost. But sometimes to make things sound better you change them. Most of what I told you was true, I said; but there was one part that I made up, one part that didn't really happen. Can you tell me what it is?

As if with one voice, they chorused back at me: That the chipmunks looked like socks!

We do not always know from where we set out when we— children or adults—set out to invent, to create, to imagine. However reflective we may become in maturity, we may never be omniscient about ourselves and our world. We can only have a limited experience of our times, our selves, our physical and spiritual and moral and psychological contexts. Our limited experience is shaped like a piece of pie, with ourselves at the point and the world in panorama as the crust beyond, out there. To the kindergartners, the world that included dying gerbils and visiting writers—whatever they are—might well include wolves conversant in the literature of late eighteenth-century chamber music. For those little kids, comparing chipmunks with balled-up socks was the most crucial imaginative leap, the challenge of a new way of thinking.

Later in the season, I went into a first-grade class in Niskayuna, New York. There was again some sort of a schedule problem; this time it had to do with a classmate who was sick but who had been brought in to the classroom, for the first time in weeks, to meet me, the guest author. The sick child wore a bandanna because her head was partly shaved following an operation on a brain tumor. During the excitement of community creation, the bandanna slipped off. The other children were too well prepared by their teacher to comment, and too involved in our story even to notice, or so I thought at first.

The teacher had read the children a book called *Bony Legs*, and I told the class another version of a Russian fairy tale with Baba Yaga the witch in it. We discussed the shape and elements of a fairy tale. Then we wrote a quick story together, with me calling for suggestions and providing a basic framework, and the kids shouting out ideas, which I scribbled on the board. In slightly bowdlerized form, here is *The Story of the Poor Potato*.

> Once upon a time there was a poor little potato named Chip. The potato was two years old and by now he was brown as a bear. But he felt sad because he was poor and he had no snowpants. Without snowpants, he thought he might get cut, and peeled, and eaten like a snack.
>
> One day Chip decided to find Baba Yaga the Witch and ask her for some help. So he rolled

and rocked, and he rocked and rolled, and sang himself a little song to soothe his soul as he went along. Then Chip saw the skeleton bones of Baba Yaga's fence. The eyes in the skulls shined like diamonds in the foggy forest. "Who is knocking on my door?" said Baba Yaga. "Chip is," said Chip. "Come in," groaned Baba Yaga. So Chip hopped in. "Whadaya want today, ya lousy vegetable?" snapped the hungry Witch. "I need snowpants," said the potato, "to keep me safe and sound from slicing and dicing." "If you jump into the fire and stay there and then jump back out, I will give you snowpants," promised the Witch. But she really wanted some potato stew, and went to the ocean for some clams and lobsters, and Chip sat down and cried and prayed and rocked and rolled and went a little nutso.

Suddenly a rain of diamonds came through the chimney and landed in the fire. When Baba Yaga got home she said, "Jump in, I see the fire is ready for roasting," because the hearth twinkled with light.

Chip flew into the fireplace and landed on the silver, white, gold, and orange diamonds, and the Witch thought that they were fire. To trick the Witch, Chip said, "Yikes, ouch, I'm frying!" Then he jumped back out. "Huh, I don't know how you did that, you should be dead by now," said the Witch. But she had to give Chip some snowpants and Chip ran home. The snowpants protected Chip for ever and ever, until they fell off. But that's another story.

It was only later, on my way home that afternoon, that I put together what had been written by the children with what they had been seeing: The shaved skull with its scars looked quite a bit like an Idaho potato. I don't believe the children thought consciously in metaphor: Amanda's head looks like a raw, unpeeled potato. But when you remember their story, you see what the children are doing, consciously or unconsciously. With the little material they have been given, they are shaping a version of experience in which the much abused potato is seen, for a time, to weather the adversity of fate, through a combination of luck and pluck. The story reveals what they are hoping for Amanda, and for themselves.

Writers tell strange things about the world. And it may not be that diamonds will ever pour in our chimneys, or even that chipmunks will ever remind us of rolled-up socks. But if we can occasionally believe that the wolves of the world sing Mozart—even only in the context of a story—we are strengthening in ourselves a habit of pluck to help us through when luck is in short supply.

These remarks were made at *Image and Word: Patterns of Creativity*, CLNE at Mount Holyoke College, South Hadley, Massachusetts, in 1994.

WORLDS APART

SUSAN COOPER

"Worlds Apart" is a powerful title to present to anyone involved in the writing of fantasy. It has a ring of The Other World, of echoes and shadows and things not quite within reach—and with those, for my metaphor-ridden mind, an implication of things unattainable or lost. One of the very first cuttings in the scrapbook I kept briefly when I was young is an article called "The Lost World," written for the Oxford University newspaper, *Cherwell*. Even at the age of nineteen I was already mourning something that was past. This article was a lament over the vanishing of magic and fairy tale. I could see my childhood vanishing into the distance and feel adulthood gobbling me up, and I wrote sorrowfully that the solitary bright spot in a dead world was Professor Tolkien's new epic, *The Lord of the Rings*. (It *was* a new epic in 1954; we were waiting for the last volume to come out.)

Well, The Lost World was so far from being lost that I was to spend the larger part of my life writing books about it, and Professor Tolkien's lonely bright spot became, of course, not only a best-seller but a kind of international cult. So much for the prescience of a nineteen-year-old. But that was in another country, and although the wench is not yet dead, she is altered. It's hard to be objective about Worlds Apart when I find myself back in Oxford, actually living here again for a few days. I came up to this university thirty-eight years ago, and it changed my life utterly. I was a naive, shy, practically mute eighteen-year-old, talented I suppose, but shackled by all the rigid insecurities of the English lower middle class. And here I was, plunged for three years into a privileged, challenging, protected hothouse of a world, and I emerged as a (relatively) confident, (relatively) grown-up writer. Oxford taught me how to write—not by giving me courses in "creative writing," perish the thought, but by teaching me how to read. Among other things.

I discovered libraries, real libraries—Bodley, the ultimate library. I discovered jazz, and sailing, and I watched Roger Bannister run the world's first four-minute mile, out at the Iffley Road track. I discovered sex, of course; I wrote a mini-thesis about Shakespeare's Treatment of Time, and I managed to become the first woman to edit the university newspaper, *Cherwell.* The last of these accomplishments was technically against the rules. If you were an Oxford undergraduate in those days—perhaps still—you had a mentor, a nanny, called your moral tutor. He or she was supposed to guide your major decisions about life, and to keep you from major error. My moral tutor was a brilliant but remote scholar, and I had heard her fulminate about a former student who had taken to publishing newspaper articles. "Marghanita is prostituting her talent!" she'd cried. And here was I wanting not only to edit the newspaper but to do it in the term before Schools, Oxford's name for final examinations. I knew that if I asked my moral tutor's permission, she would say no—so I didn't ask. I just did it. And luckily she never read the newspaper, so she never knew.

I then went off to become a journalist for seven years, and

I'm not sure she ever knew that either. But eventually when I was thirty-two I sent her a copy of *The Dark Is Rising,* and she wrote a nice letter back saying she'd always thought I had promise. Perhaps she liked the fact that I had tucked inside the story a quotation from the line written in Anglo-Saxon around King Alfred's Jewel, the greatest treasure of Oxford's Ashmolean Museum.

I dare say everyone looks back at some period in life as a golden time. Oxford was mine. And I *knew* it, at the time, which was an uncommon extra blessing. I would find myself waking up in the morning, or pulling on my gown, or walking down that amazing curve of the High Street, and hearing a small amazed voice in my head saying, *"I'm at Oxford."* Whatever might go wrong, however agonizing the love affair, however unnerving the examination, *I was at Oxford.* I've never felt so lucky, worked so hard and had so much fun, all at once.

And the golden world still hangs there in memory, shining, because it never had to acquire any dents or tarnish. Seven years after I came down from Oxford I married an American and moved to the U.S.A., and I've never spent a night in this university or city since—until last night. For my contemporaries who stayed in Britain, there was familiar old Oxford, still chugging away, eighty miles from London, changing yet remaining the same. It was connected at least tenuously to the fabric of their everyday lives, and if they didn't become dons themselves they knew people who did, or—in due course—they acquired children who started going up to do their own degrees. But for me Oxford was, is, in a time warp: It remains the magical world I entered just after my eighteenth birthday, and left just after my twenty-first. I can never go back to that world, even though here I am in Oxford now. Yet it isn't lost. It changed me, and so it is *in here* rather than *out there*. It's just—set apart.

For that is the powerful word, in our title. Apart. The Other World that's of value, in children's literature—or any other kind of literature, for that matter—doesn't have to be a shadowy fairyland, or a distant childhood. It is simply a world set apart. Separated, by geography or imagination. When we go into it, in the beginning, we have no idea of what we're doing. A reading child goes into a favorite story, which is read over and over again, as if he kept returning to a favorite place. He may indeed have a physical place as well: a corner of a room behind a curtain or a chair, or whatever. Some safe child-sized space, which may be of vast importance to him when he's four, even though he may not remember a thing about it when he's fourteen. It can be anywhere.

For the English author Alan Garner this separate space was, of all things, a ceiling. He had three long serious illnesses when he was a child, diphtheria, meningitis, and pneumonia, and so he spent months and years on his back in bed. Being both imaginative and ill, for much of the time he lived in the imaginary landscape he saw in the plaster above him; in its forest and hills, its cloudy sky, the road leading to its horizon. That was his world, and it molded his future. It's important to remember, as Garner says, that as children we accept our own circumstances as normality, having no concept of "things being other than they are found to be."

When I was about six years old, in wartime England, my brother and I were given a collection of cigarette cards, which had been put together by a friend of our parents in that mysterious world known as Before the War. (We were always hearing about Before the War: It was a vanished wonderland of freedom and plenty, filled with things we had never seen, like fountains and bananas.) A cigarette card was a picture, the size of a visiting card: a promotional gimmick that came in a packet of cigarettes. There were sets of them, so that people had to

smoke themselves to death in order to acquire the cards to complete a set. Our favorite set showed an assortment of fantasy
means of transport—and there was one card in particular that
I came back to again and again.

The picture on this card showed a one-person vehicle, a
huge glass sphere. I suppose it was a sphere within a sphere,
because it rolled itself along and yet remained upright: The picture showed it bowling merrily through a field, with its lucky
owner sitting inside, in the driver's seat. And as well as a seat, I
always felt, he had in there a bed, a table, a stove, presumably
even a mini-bathroom. All mod con. The sphere was a mobile
home, a little round house. A little world.

I had dreams about that great glass ball. I would roll
through life in it, in my dreams, self-contained, protected, safe.
I was a very fearful child, as I remember, and the glass sphere—
being, presumably, unbreakable—seemed to me to offer the
perfect combination of independence, adventurousness and
invulnerability. I knew it didn't exist, but I longed for it, fer-
vently. Perhaps it would be invented by the time I grew up; perhaps I should find it waiting for me, in the future. I was too
young to analyze my passion for this object, of course, which
was just as well. You could hardly find a more striking example
of the desire to return to the womb. And yet, perhaps there was
more to it than that. . . .

A great many children find an equivalent of my rolling glass
sphere, I think. Without knowing quite what they're doing,
they put themselves inside a protective vehicle that will help
them get through life without being damaged. It isn't round,
however, it's generally rectangular; made not of glass but of
paper. Many printed pages, between two hard covers. Or these
days, more likely soft covers. While children are inside it, reading, they have left the real world and are living in another. They
have escaped. But if they are lucky, there's something else hap-

pening as well. They may be changed, just a little, by living in this world apart. They may take back a talisman from it, some small buried insight or idea that will stay with them forever, and help them in the hard matter of understanding and surviving their own world. It makes me think of that wonderful old comprehensive Everyman's Library published in the early years of this century by Dent and Dutton. The series encompassed all the best books in every field—or what Dent's editor Ernest Rhys thought were the best—and on the endpapers of each book was a quotation that could have been the book talking to its reader.

> Everyman, I will go with thee
> To be thy guide;
> In thy most need
> To be at thy side.

In the old morality play of Everyman those words are given to the character named Knowledge. We all need *him*, Lord knows.

One of the best things about the old Everyman books must have been their friendly size, which made them almost as portable as the modern paperback. My grandfather used to keep one in his pocket, so that he could dive inside it whenever he had a spare moment. This was good for his head, though it didn't do great things for his jackets. And now that we do have paperbacks, you can see Grandad's modern counterparts in buses and underground trains today, to some extent in the United States but more often in Britain, and above all in Japan: rows of travelers, sitting or standing, each reading a book, each inside his or her own little bubble of story.

When my children were young I particularly liked watching them reading in airplanes, on long transatlantic flights: There they sat, doubly encapsulated, held inside this cocoon of pressurized air zipping across the waves at 350 miles an hour, but within *that* held too in another cocoon, woven by a writer's imagination.

On the whole, our motives for reading are probably more admirable when we're children than after we've grown up. Yes, the child is often retreating into a cocoon—but more often than not he or she is on a voyage of discovery, seeking out new worlds. Not us: We tend to look for the familiar. We know what we like. In the universe of books there are numbers of solar systems out there and most people stay firmly within one of them; they stick with thrillers, for instance, or biographies, or big meaty novels, the five-hundred-pagers spanning several generations.

The worlds within this last category, the big realistic novels, are true microcosms: filled with recognizable people and situations that will draw the reader in, make him (or her) smile or shiver, laugh or cry just as the people and situations do—less often—in his own life. They are more colorful than his own life, and they have the great virtue of being unreal, so that he gets all this lovely vicarious experience without any headaches: pleasure without responsibility. He joins the book's family—just for a little while. It's not unlike the experience of becoming part of an instant, temporary family at a Children's Literature New England institute. The enclosed, focused world of a conference can gobble you up, producing a sort of miniature hothouse version of the stresses and affections and dilemmas of the larger everyday world. Like the totally engaging novel whose plot you will forget in a month, it doesn't last, but it has its own intense valuable vitality while it's happening.

This phenomenon reaches its most extreme form in the performing arts, as anyone knows who has lived through the full production process of a play, opera or ballet, or the shooting of a film. I've seldom been on a film set for more than a few days at a time, but once I was on location for the whole six-week shoot of a television film I'd written: part of the instant family, living through a ferocious range of human emotion from fury to love and back again. I have on my wall a souvenir of that time, a poster signed by all the members of the crew, with the most fulsome, fervent messages. "I shall never forget working with you. . . ." they say. "Thank you for the most wonderful experience of my life. . . ." To my buddy, with great love and respect. . . ." And I look at all the names of these people to whom I was so devoted, in our tight enclosed six-week world years ago, and I can hardly remember a thing about any one of them. Just as they probably remember nothing about me. If I had met them inside the world of a novel, at least I could reread the book.

But the slice-of-life novel is really not so much a world apart as an interlude—like the conference or the film set, the holiday hotel or the voyage by sea or air. You enter it, you live there for a while, you leave again. Perhaps it will alter you; usually it will not. I suspect that the book that takes you into a world apart must also *trouble* you, at least a little. And the troubling stays with you, like the grit in the oyster, and afterward you are changed.

Consider, for instance, Ursula Le Guin's novel *Very Far Away from Anywhere Else,* a lovely book, though not perhaps the one that first springs to people's minds when they hear Mrs. Le Guin's name. This is a book about apartness. About Owen who is seventeen and amazingly good at math and science, and Natalie who is an eighteen-year-old musician and composer. They each have something that makes them different from everyone around them. Adolescence, as Owen says in the book, is the age "when kids begin to turn into people, and find out they are alone"—and react in a way that's not friendly to individualists.

"I think what you mostly do when you find you really are alone is to panic," Owen says.

You rush to the opposite extreme and pack yourself into groups—clubs, teams, societies, types. You suddenly start dressing exactly like the others. It's a way of being invisible. The way you sew the patches on the holes in your blue jeans becomes incredibly important. If you do it wrong you're not with it. That's a peculiar phrase, you know? With it. With what? With them. With the others. All together. Safety in numbers. I'm not me. I'm a basketball letter. I'm a popular kid. I'm my friend's friend. I'm a black leather growth on a Honda. I'm a member. I'm a teenager. You can't see me, all you can see is us. We're safe.

And if We see You standing alone by yourself, if you're lucky we'll ignore you. If you're not lucky, we might throw rocks. Because we don't like people standing there with the wrong kind of patches on their jeans reminding us that we're each alone and none of us is safe.

You stand there with any kind of patches on your jeans today and they may throw rocks, because this book was published in 1976 and today—in my part of America, at any rate—patches aren't with it, unpatched holes are with it. Which just goes to prove what Mrs. Le Guin's Owen was saying.

Very Far Away from Anywhere Else is a kind of poem: a beautiful eighty-nine-page story about the way two people learn to cope with the fact that they must each live in a world apart from everyone else, if they are to fulfill the promise that is in them. I suppose it appeals to everyone who has ever had to survive a sensation of being different. (There was more than one reason why I wanted, when young, to roll through life inside that protective glass ball.) It is full of images that might well echo through this institute.

Haworth Parsonage, for instance.

> *Wuthering Heights* was Natalie's favorite book [says
> Owen], and she knew a lot about the Brontë fam-
> ily, these four genius children living in a vicarage
> on a moor in the middle of Nowhere, England, a
> hundred and fifty years ago. Talk about being iso-
> lated! I read a biography of them she gave me, and
> I realized that maybe I thought I had been lonely,
> but my life had been an orgy of sociability, com-
> pared to those four.

The Brontë family as a world apart: Ursula Le Guin presents it to us on a plate, and we should keep it on our table this
week. Then she moves on. On to Thorn, an invented country
that Owen lives in as the Brontë children lived in theirs—in his
imagination—during the years when he is changing from a
child to a young adult. He says, of Thorn,

> It started out as a kingdom when I was twelve,
> but by the time I was fifteen or sixteen it had
> become a kind of free socialistic set-up, and so I
> had to work out all the history of how they got
> from autocracy to socialism, and also their rela-
> tionships to other countries. They weren't at all
> friendly with Russia, China or the United States.
> In fact they traded only with Switzerland, Swe-
> den and the Republic of San Marino. . . . Thorn
> was a very small country, on an island in the
> South Atlantic, only about sixty miles across, and
> a very long way away from anywhere else. . . .

Natalie is writing a wind quintet for Thorn, by the end of

the book. She helps Owen come to terms with his necessary apartness, not least through sharing awareness of her own. Perhaps this is really a book about talent and the acceptance of it, and the fact that learning how to work is one of the best ways of learning how to live. Natalie knows, and Owen recognizes, that she is set apart by her music. He says, of some songs she has written, "That's the way you really talk."

"Owen, you are the neatest person I ever knew," she says. "Nobody else understands that. I don't even know any other musicians who understand that. I can't really say anything. I can't even really be anything. Except in music. Maybe later. Maybe when I get good at music, maybe when I learn how to do that, then I'll be able to do some of the rest, too. Maybe I'll even become a human being."

And the two of them launch into adult life, and into the paradox that it's easier to survive apartness if you are connected to someone else. That even if the other person isn't actually around all the time, loving can carry you through the empty separate air, like the air pressure that keeps a fifty-ton airplane flying like a bird.

This is an achingly real book, but not an interlude. I wonder sometimes about the reactions of the children who read it. For any who feel even remotely akin to Owen and Natalie, it must be a glowing discovery. For the rest, who care more about having their jeans look the same as everyone else's jeans, I hope it's at least a little troubling. I hope it stays with them. Like the grit in the oyster, which is the necessary ingredient for—I quote from the motto of this institute—"the comprehension of the self by the detour of the comprehension of the other."

On the face of it, the clearest example of a world apart is a book of fantasy. It separates the reader from reality, and takes him or her way apart, into magic. In the kind of fantasy that begins in an apparently normal world, there is a distinct moment when this shift takes place, like a signpost saying This Way Out. It's the moment when E. Nesbit's children find the Psammead, in *Five Children and It,* or when the Phoenix hatches from its egg in *The Phoenix and the Carpet;* when Alice goes through the looking-glass, when Lewis's children go through the wardrobe, or when Alan Garner's Roland walks through a door in a ruined Manchester church and is suddenly standing among the boulders at the foot of a cliff in the land of Elidor.

Or my favorite paragraph in *The Children of Green Knowe,* when Mrs. Oldknow tells small Tolly that the three children whose portraits are on the walls, with whose lives he is so fascinated, all died with their mother three hundred years ago in the Great Plague, leaving their old grandmother bereft.

> Mrs. Oldknow said, "It sounds very sad to say they all died, but it didn't really make so much difference. I expect the old grandmother soon found out they were still here."
>
> Tolly was watching something travelling across the floor towards him. It was a marble, a glass one with coloured spirals in the middle. It stopped by his listless fingers. He picked it up. It was warm.

There's a moment that crosses this same kind of boundary in my own book *The Dark Is Rising,* when the boy Will is carried away by a white horse from a danger not yet named, and the horse, galloping through the countryside, takes off and rides up into the sky. Into fantasy. I love those moments when we are transported into another world—which is no doubt why I write the kind of fantasy that contains them. It's probably related to another obsession of mine that I'm forever using as an analogy: that breathtaking moment in the theater when the house lights have gone down, the voices have hushed, and the curtain begins to go up. Into fantasy.

(I have to add that I was almost cured of this obsession once when I was standing at the back of the stalls for a performance of a play I'd written, and as the house lights began to dim, my companion said in my ear, "Just think—it's like eight hundred people opening a book of yours, all at once." And I found this image so terrifying that I had to leave, instantly. Eight hundred books are much more frightening than one stage. At least in the theater you have the chance of blaming the actors, if people don't like the play.)

Fantasy writers born in America tend, for whatever reason, to be more direct than those born in Britain. They take you straight to their world apart: From the first page, you are not in our own world but in Ursula Le Guin's Earthsea, Anne McCaffrey's Pern, Lloyd Alexander's Prydain. Or for that matter, just to disprove my own generalization about nationality, Professor Tolkien's Middle-earth. This brand of fantasy could be said to be the ultimate in separation: How much further from reality can you get than to be in a different universe, a different time, belonging to a different species?

But it's an illusion. Fantasy, of whatever kind, may seem to be picking you up and carrying you away, but in fact it's taking you right back home. All fantasy involves metaphor. I once called a piece I'd written about it "Escaping into Ourselves"— and that's precisely what we're doing in this kind of fiction, both of us, writer and reader. The writer takes the images, themes, characters that come bubbling up from his—or her—unconscious mind (the ultimate world apart), and puts them into his story. There they stay, part of the fabric, and like radioactive elements they give off signals about the meaning of the story, the

nature of its metaphor. But because they come from the unconscious, the writer himself generally doesn't know what these signals are. He may not even know they are there.

Quite often the reader doesn't know either. But his—or
her—own unconscious mind has its own little Geiger counter.
Ticking away as he reads, it picks up these signals from the story
and takes them in, without the reader having consciously recognized them at all. This is a totally nonrational process. It has
nothing to do with critical judgments; it's as instinctive and
uncontrollable as being in love. The rational mind, probably
adult, may read Mary Norton's books about those very small
creatures the Borrowers in a thoroughly objective manner. It
will admire the ingenuity that turns a nutshell into a cup, a
soapdish into a dinghy, a knitting-needle into a punt-pole. It will
be entertained by the story, and draw parallels with Gulliver and
the Lilliputians. But it won't necessarily make the instinctive
unconscious connection through which the child reader, being
small, understands that these are books about the tensions and
delights of living as a small person in a large world. The analyt-
ical mind makes more noise than the imagination. It drowns out
those signals from the unconscious. Children, today, make the
best readers of fantasy, because children, as C. S. Lewis
observed a long time ago, read only to enjoy.

I am a jack-of-all-trades, as an author; I've spent thirty years
responding, probably unwisely, to the challenges of different
forms. But fantasy is my natural habitat. It's the kind of writing
I am best at, I think. I've seldom deliberately chosen it; it simply
tends to take over. The first book I wrote that was published for
children didn't set out to be a fantasy at all; it was supposed to
be an adventure story, but magic began glimmering through it
before I had reached the end of Chapter Two. This has been
happening at intervals ever since, as if my imagination were
refusing ever to rely on straightforward reality. Often, when I

begin to think about an idea for a book, it's as though I were sitting at a concert, hearing a new orchestral piece of music; I relax into the sweep of strings and woodwind, percussion and brass, convinced that I am listening to the first theme of the first movement of a symphony. But sooner or later, soft as faraway bells, the notes of the piano come creeping in. There's the same theme, simple, crystalline, then growing, growing until great chords are crashing away and intertwining with the orchestra—and lo, after all it's not a symphony, yet again it's a concerto. With fantasy as the solo instrument, taking over the piece of music, making its very specific magic. Showing off, you might say.

Why? Why is it that my imagination, my world apart, chooses to express itself fully only in fantasy? Penelope Farmer grappled with the question in a talk about form, seventeen years ago; she said, "I am asked why, as a writer for children, I do not produce nice, solid, useful novels on the problem of the adopted child, or aimed at the reluctant reader, and so forth, instead of highly symbolic (according to some reviewers) obscure (according to others)—anyway, *difficult* fantasies. Very simply, because I cannot. It is the same for everyone—no one can express himself effectively except in ways and forms suited to him. . . ." When she tried to write in other, more realistic forms, she said,

> I lose the simplest verbal competence. . . . Whereas writing within my usual form, fantasy, given time and given a good idea, I feel sometimes a kind of fluency and ease. And as for form, I scarcely have to look for it. . . . It pushes up from some unknown part of my mind, I can feel it happening, watch it slowly, gradually, fall neatly into place.
>   . . . It seems that I need symbols and images. . . . Without those images, I cannot frame my idea and expand it into narrative. . . . For me the extra-

ordinary is a means of looking at people sideways
and finding out more about them—and me.

Which is another way of saying that she, and I, are escaping into ourselves. Writing is one of the loneliest professions in
the world because it has to be practiced in this very separate
private world, in *here*. Not in the mind; in the imagination. And
I think it is possible that the writing of fantasy is the loneliest
job of the lot, since you have to go further inside. You have to
make so close a connection with the unconscious that the
unbiddable door will open and the images fly out, like birds. It's
not unlike writing poetry.

It makes you superstitious. Most writers indulge in small
private rituals to start themselves writing each day, and I find
that when I'm working on a fantasy I'm even more ludicrously
twitchy than usual. The very first half hour at the desk has nothing much to do with fantasy or even ritual: It's what J. B. Priest-
ley used to call "sharpening pencils"—the business of doing
absolutely everything you can think of to put off the moment of
starting work. You make another cup of coffee. You find a tele-
phone call that must be made, a letter that must be answered.
You *do* sharpen pencils. You look at the plant on the windowsill
and decide this is just the time to water it, or fertilize it, or prune
it. Maybe it's even time to repot it. You hunt for the houseplant
book, and look this up, and it says severely that this kind of plant
enjoys being pot-bound and should never be repotted. So you
turn to the bowl of paper clips on the desk, and find that safety
pins and pennies and buttons have found their way in, so of
course you really ought to sort out the paper clips. . . .

Finally guilt drives you to the manuscript—and that's when
the real ritual begins. (I should go back to the first person,
because in this respect everyone's different.) I have to start by
reading. I read a lot of what I've already written, probably two

or three chapters, even though I already know it all by heart. I read the notes I made to myself the day before when I stopped writing—those were the end-of-the-day ritual, to help with the starting of the next. During this process I've picked up one of the toys scattered around my study, and my fingers are half-consciously playing with it: a shell, a smooth sea-washed pebble from an island beach, a chunky ceramic owl from Sweden, a little stone wombat from Australia. I read the last chapter again. I wander to a bookshelf and read a page of something vaguely related to my fantasy: Eliot's *Quartets*, maybe, or de la Mare's notes to *Come Hither.* I have even been known to blow bubbles, from a little tube that sits on my desk, and to sit staring at the colors that swirl over their brief surfaces. This is the moment someone else usually chooses to come into the room, and I can become very irritable if they don't appreciate that they are observing a writer seriously at work.

What I'm doing, of course, is taking myself out of the world I'm in, and trying to find my way back into the world apart. Once I've managed that, I am inside the book that I'm writing, and am *seeing* it, so vividly that I do not see what I'm actually staring at: the wall, or the typewriter, or the tree outside the window. I suppose it is a variety of trance state, though that's a perilous word. It makes one think of poor Coleridge, waking from an opium-induced sleep with two hundred glowing lines of *Kubla Khan* in his head, being interrupted by a person from Porlock when he'd written down only about ten of them, and finding, when the person had gone, that he'd forgotten all the rest. Trance is fragile.

The world of the imagination is not fragile, not once you've reached it, but because it is set apart you can never be *sure* of reaching it. It seems very curious to be standing here in the university that tried to teach me reason, and confessing to uncertainty and superstition of a kind that would have appalled my tutor. Reason, however, is singularly unhelpful to a novelist except in a few specialized situations, like the matter of choosing a publisher, or arguing points of English grammar with a copy editor. The imagination is not reasonable—or tangible, or visible, or obedient. It's an island out in the ocean, which often seems to retreat as you sail toward it. Sometimes it vanishes altogether, mirage-like, and nothing can be done to bring it back within reach. This produces a bad day during which you write nothing of value and have to wait till tomorrow and start again.

We cast spells to find our way into the unconscious mind, and the imagination that lives there, because we know that's the only way to get into a place where magic is made. "Open sesame!" I am shouting, silently, desperately to the door of my imagination, as I play with the pebble I found on a distant island beach, as I stare at the wall.

Our readers believe that the process is magical too. That's why they say to us in that bemused, incredulous, faintly envious way, "Where do you get your ideas?" It always sounds like a dinner guest contemplating the salad, asking a hostess to reveal the name of some special shop. "Where do you get your tomatoes?"

The answer might well be the same whether it's tomatoes or ideas. "I grow them. In my garden." If the subject is ideas, they know that it's a magic garden. They've been there, transported to it while they read the book. Though they didn't have to go through all the same palaver to get there that we did; all they had to do was to open the cover. They come into this place by reading words on paper, nothing more. They've been transported to separate worlds before in the theater, or the cinema, sometimes even in front of the television set, but there they were witnessing reproductions of things happening, watching actors, through the fourth wall. In the book, the magic is all in the words on paper, taking them into the writer's imagination. Words on paper. Isn't that extraordinary? The Russian director Aleksandr Sokurov just made a new film of *Madame Bovary,* and spoke of it with proper but uncommon humility. "The film is the child of literature and not the father," he said, in an interview. "It will never be able to replace the silent and private dialogue between reader and book."

Six weeks ago I was speaking at another children's book conference, a long way away, called "Literature and Hawaii's Children." It took place on the island of Oahu and then, a smaller repeat performance, on Hawaii, also known as The Big Island. This is the home of Pele, goddess of fire, and two of the world's most active volcanoes: Mauna Loa, which had a spectacular eruption in 1984, and Kilauea, which has been erupting continuously since 1983. My editor, Margaret McElderry, was with me, and on our one day off she came to me, bright-eyed, waving a leaflet that advertised helicopter flights over the volcano Kilauea.

I looked at the leaflet, and I thought very superstitious thoughts about the goddess Pele. "I can't afford it," I said.

Margaret McElderry is a strong-minded lady. She said, "We're going. I didn't give you a birthday present this year. This is it."

So up we went in a helicopter, over the dead black lava fields stretching to the sea, over steaming cracks and vents, over huge creeping fingers of new hot lava—suitably called in Hawaiian, which is a language full of hesitations, *'a'a.* To the crater, around which—and into which—we swooped like a small rash bird.

The helicopter felt like a sturdy little refuge, but it grew warm. I was so busy taking photographs, and peering through the smoke and fumes at the glowing red heart of the volcano, that I didn't hear the echoes that were beginning to murmur out of my unconscious mind.

Then we banked away from the crater, and up through ragged white cliffs and valleys of cloud. Away from the urgency of the volcano, through this tranquil, mounded sky, with glimpses of black and eventually green fields beneath our feet. They were *literally* beneath our feet; I looked down past my shoes to see them. It was a very small helicopter, and we were sitting surrounded by glass in its nose, next to the pilot. There was glass on either side of us and in front of us, glass above us and glass below us.

I had seen this before, somewhere, a long time ago.

It was as if we were sitting inside a glass ball.

If you have the cast of mind of a fantasy writer, and if you pay attention to the life you are living, once in a while you will find yourself bang in the middle of a metaphor. Here I was, suddenly inside the huge glass sphere that had haunted me when I was young. Inside the picture from the cigarette card.

I was in my world apart: the writer's imagination, the child's book. But I knew more about its value now than I had before. It wasn't an escape really, nor a refuge. It stood for freedom, and discovery, and wonder. The best thing about it wasn't that it was safe, but that it was *flying*.

These remarks were made at *Worlds Apart*, CLNE at Oxford University, Oxford, England, in 1992.

DREAMING A MYTHIC WORLD

PAT O'SHEA

The first idea I had for *The Hounds of the Morrigan* came in a dream: a good omen, you might think, for a myth-associated story. In the dream, my son — who was then six years old — used a little silver bow and arrow to kill a terrible giant. I dreamt that this giant terrorized a whole country — one without boundaries but magically separated from other countries — and the most horrifying thing about him was that he couldn't be killed. In my dream I saw him appear to die many times, to fall lifelessly to the ground where his shadow broke into pieces. Each time that he fell in death, the shadow gradually pulled together until it was again whole. As soon as the shadow was complete, the giant was alive. The shadow was his soul — the thing that animated him.

But in my dream, when my little son Jimmy killed the giant, part of the giant's shadow fell into a pot of soup where it melted. His soul was incomplete and this time he was dead for good the way we usually are! When I woke up, I knew that I had dreamt a fairy tale, and that one day I would write it. I decided then that the giant would be the Glomach.

The Glomach was an old enemy from my childhood days.

He was not, to my knowledge, part of the old Irish mythology with which I was familiar from my school days and later reading. I believe that he was entirely the creation of the mothers, the grandmothers, or great-grandmothers—the myth makers—in the little city where I grew up. I was told that he lived down Biddy's Lane and that if I didn't come in when I was called on winters' nights, he'd get me. In those days there was almost no motorized traffic on the roads and it was safe for children to play out. We particularly loved the winter when it got dark early and everything seemed different and magical under the streetlights—and if there was a frost we threw buckets of water on the road to freeze and make a slide. Of course our mothers had to get us to bed so that we could get a good night's sleep. We had to get up for school in the morning, after all. Hence the Glomach: our bogeyman. I have never heard of him in any other setting or read of him in any book. But he was surely part of my mythology in childhood, a metaphor for evil and danger.

Significantly, he didn't exist for us in daylight. We would happily play house in the forsaken and ruined cottages that ran down one side of Biddy's Lane as far as the nuns' field.

It's odd that other children had different perceptions of him. I've been checking this recently and I find that to my eldest sister—who was sixteen, already grown up, when I was born—he was the gentleman with cloven hoofs who tried to entice those who were out very late and were a bit squiffy to a game of cards in Blake's Lane: the devil. I had heard of this gentlemen as an entirely separate entity. To my cousins Angela and Davey he was also the devil, disguised as a big black dog. I wonder if he is the same big black dog with burning eyes that followed my mother when she was young, up the hill at Grealish Town, with his hot breath hitting the calves of her legs. And could that be the evening that she saw the woman sitting on the rock in the middle of the Sandy River combing her long hair and moaning like the banshee that she was? Oh, there were many stories, as much a part of our lives as the shoes on our feet!—part of the armory of our myth-creating mothers.

So the Glomach was the first character that suggested himself for the story. And given what I have just been saying about the strange tales and mythic creatures and stories with which I had grown up, to think about the characters of my dream in the context of those tales seemed therefore natural enough—they offered rich possibilities for its development, both in genre and settings.

To combine myth and fantasy with wild humor and poetic beauty seemed perfectly natural also. Less usual perhaps in the Anglo-Saxon fantasy tradition, grotesque and farcical humor has been a striking element in the Irish written and vernacular tradition, going back as far as the hero tales and myths themselves.

So when I was actually writing *The Hounds of the Morrigan*, figures from the Irish mythology of my schoolbooks—Angus Óg, the goddess Brigit, the tripartite goddess of death and destruction known as the Mórrígan, the hero Cúchulain, and Cathbad, the druid—these figures suggested themselves naturally and pleasingly for supernatural protagonists. And the story itself formed in my imagination in the traditional quest form, with its oppositions of good and evil, love and hate, peace and war, life and death on the epic scale. Its heroes too were the traditional types of innocence in fairy tales, a small boy and a small girl, who must go through trials of their courage to find knowledge of themselves and of what they could be, and in so doing gain a vital sense of their individual worth and importance, however weak they might appear against the powers they encountered.

The actual mythology the book uses is very selective and fragmentary, if one were looking for a recreation of the Irish gods of the hero tales—it mingles faithfulness to a mythical basis with wholly individual recreations of character and events. The hounds of the title are not in the actual mythology. The Dagda is not really the father of moral goodness in the hero tales so much as a fertility god, the source of creative bounty, of energy and powers. The Mórrígan was Skald Crow and the Queen of Phantoms *only* and no laughing matter at all. Queen Maeve was the cause of her own children's deaths through her crazed infatuation for the white bull of Cooley and the war through which she sought to possess him, but she was never to my knowledge an old woman walking the roads tormented by half-remembered dreams and an unexplained misery, and accompanied always by her own little rain cloud of depression and sadness and a troop of blathering ducks. In her rightful original being, Queen Maeve would have made Margaret Thatcher look like Pollyanna.

Likewise, the gods Brigit and Angus Óg and the semi-divine Cúchulain never appeared as they do in the transformations in my book, but they were all heroes or gods or supernatural beings in our Irish myths, about whose deeds and attributes I had read in my schoolbooks and later in Lady Gregory, and who could play a useful, exemplary, protective and inspirational part in this new myth (I suppose) of my own. . . .

So what were the underlying attractions of the mythical framework? What was the resulting personal myth a metaphor about? Can one say?

Perhaps it is not really possible, except to ruminate upon some of the almost inextricable and irreducible motives and intimations—glimpses of understanding—that I sense as I reread the book. A sense that myth reflects an elemental need in human beings and distills our feelings of what life involves— perhaps of how it ought to be. A sense that the need to make and tell significant stories comes from that same deep-rooted human need for shape and meaning. The wish to commemorate things. To experience things again through reflection and fantasy. To share experience and wonders—particularly in my case the wonders of seeing things with the fresh eyes of childhood. The wish to create something that will absorb and nourish children in the way I feel my childhood (and adulthood, come to that) have been nourished by the magical world of the imagination—with its freedom from the limitations of our constructed everyday lives, its powers to transport and transcend, to take us out of ourselves into a timeless and "other" world. And, importantly from the practical view of creating a rich and enriching story, the scope that a mythic framework gives—to do all these things.

As children read—myths and fiction alike—they learn about the dangers of the world, but ultimately in a safe and strengthening way, a way that tells them that weak and vulnerable as they may be, they can nevertheless win through, survive the losses and pain, and learn that they and their own lives are of value, have importance, that they make a difference to the world and to the life around them—if they have the courage, and, sometimes, good fortune. In fiction, there can be a reinforcement for children reading about a world in which goodness and kindness are not totally overwhelmed and defeated, even if they have to go through great epic dangers, disappointments, reverses, and are never securely triumphant.

Children can be made to feel powerless also, of little consequence, even worthless. They can have fears and uncertainties and a sense of not being in control of their lives. They may sometimes find the world hostile, a place in which domination is the rule and where cunning or manipulation or force are the ways to bend the world to their will.

It could be helpful to get children to feel that the limitations on their power in the world are *not* threatening—that they can still find freedom within themselves; that even though they cannot control, they can influence things; that it is possible (even essential) to live with uncertainty, to live by faith, to choose their own values and keep by them whatever the pressures and forces against them. If they keep faith, trust themselves and their judgment, they will come through.

Life and growing involve meeting one's own fears and doubts, so children should be nurtured to have a belief in themselves. The traditional quest-myth story in which they can identify with its hero or heroine in all the difficulties, dangers, and triumphs of the quest has still much to offer. Myths are primal acts of imagination that allow children to experience realities without being demoralized by them. Myths give children the courage to handle trauma and pain and difficulty and to retain their sense of wonder and value, and, even more, to find their lives significant.

And the writing of the story? A waking dream—for getting lost in the imagination is a waking dream—and "in dreams begin responsibility," as Yeats said. I wonder if the ancient Irish dreamed the myths?

These remarks were made at *Writing the World: Myth as Metaphor*, CLNE at Trinity College, Dublin, Ireland, in 1995.

ILLUSTRATION REPRINTED WITH PERMISSION OF PAULINE BAYNES

POLAR BEARS AND LEMMINGS

BETTY LEVIN

"The bear went over the mountain to see what it could see. . . ." Like the bear's journey, the song is circular. Thus it patterns life's journey — in part.

And something besides curiosity got the bear started — another bear invading its territory, a scarcity of prey, a hunter, a housing project, or an oil pipeline. When song and story take over, motives change. Ennobling occurs. Words like destiny and quest and pilgrimage creep in.

Bears, people, lemmings — all the species that periodically or sporadically move on — begin their journeys without much volition. We humans begin life's journey under orders we seldom understand. Before we know it, we are obeying certain instincts or drives. Yet our story-making concerns itself with reason and striving and determination.

"The animal does not reason," writes Ursula Le Guin. "And it acts 'rightly,' appropriately. It is the animal who knows the way, the way home. It is the animal within us, the dark brother, the shadow soul, which is the guide."

Consider now two such guides, one the polar bear, the other

the lemming. A century and a half after the Hudson Bay Company built a fort on the north shore of the mouth of the Churchill River, Canada acquired the area and moved the settlement to the west side. The move placed the settlement of Churchill in the migratory path of the region's polar bears.

The arctic and sub-arctic polar bear is at the top of the food chain. Every fall the bears congregate in the area to await the formation of sea ice. As soon as it can hold them, they set off for the winter, hunting seal while the ice slowly drifts south. In the summer when the ice melts, the bears land and make their way north to await the fall freeze-up. Summer is a lean time. By fall the bears are hungry.

But bears don't compose epics. They weren't heroes to the people who feared them. They weren't martyrs either. They were just dangerous critters or valuable fur or handsome trophies. So on they came, year after year, just as they had since the last ice age. It was a journey into near extinction, until the slaughter was stopped in 1973.

Every fall bears caused damage and sometimes killed people, and so every year more bears were shot. The most curious, the most persistent foragers, the strongest and boldest, the most protective mothers — these were the likely targets. If polar bears had a saga literature, their epic heroes would be those that were killed off. The bears were programmed to make the journey, and like the bear going over the mountain in the song, the journey was circular and is continuous.

Lemmings, on the other hand, are at the bottom of the food chain in the arctic. Their migrations have become symbols of mass hysteria and mass suicide. In this ecosystem, arctic foxes follow the bears and scavenge their kills. They also prey on birds and lemmings. When the bear population is stable, the arctic fox population tends to rise and the lemming population to decrease. When disease introduced by people and dogs decimates the fox population or when the number of seals and consequently polar bears declines, lemmings multiply at such a rate that they literally eat themselves out of house and home. They take off by the millions. Birds gorging on them upset their own population, so that when the lemming population crashes, the next generations of birds starve.

This sketchy picture is presented to remind us of the biological basis of human migration. We need to consider how singers of songs and tellers of tales envisioned such movements as epic journeys. We need to understand why the marauding polar bear is likely to be viewed as magnificent—and why the mousy lemming, more voracious for its size than any polar bear, conveys no sense of grandeur.

The way we perceive the polar bear and the lemming is due in part to the difference between predator and prey. Traditionally the predator is the warrior. Our warrior ethic was formed in ancient times when a test of strength meant single combat at the ford in the river or bloody battles with slingshots and spears and swords.

The history of European peoples of the prehistoric and early historic periods shows successive occupations of the continent. In its earliest accounts, the mythologizing of migrations began to transform the brutal necessities of mass movements into hero tales and quests. We have only to glance at the recent history of our own westward movement to find a small scale pattern of this sort. Manifest Destiny justifies the seizing of territory from its previous inhabitants.

The Celtic hordes, called barbarians by the Greeks and Romans, migrated across Europe, east to west. When they could move no farther and new waves of Celtic peoples swept across the continent, the previous inhabitants were either destroyed, enslaved, integrated, or driven underground.

Celtic mythology, elements of which survive through

Arthurian legends and folk history and abound in children's literature, made heroes and martyrs of tribal deities. The final Eurasian surge of peoples, out of the east and eventually into the British Isles and Ireland, are the storied People of the Goddess Danu. These people left their name on the great rivers of Europe—the Danube, Don, and Dnieper. They brought the art of magic and poetry into Britain and Ireland. Their surviving legends tell of a deal made with the Sons of Mil, the Gaels, who journeyed through Egypt, Crete, Sicily, and Spain, probably as desperate and hungry as lemmings on the run.

When the Sons of Mil reached the green land of what was to become Ireland, they moved in. The land, this last land, was divided between them and the People of the Goddess Danu, who were compelled to take the nether region—beneath mountains, burial mounds, and subterranean springs. In *The Grey King*, Susan Cooper's sleepers under the mountain are direct descendants of this mythical arrangement.

While the People of the Goddess Danu, who became fairies and boggarts and moorchildren, ruled the otherworld of death and life in death, the Sons of Mil strived to possess the land.

Out of these migrations came some of the earliest poetry in what would evolve into the language we speak today. The mythic poet of the Sons of Mil laid claim to the land by becoming one with it: "I am the wind on sea / I am ocean wave / I am Roar of Sea / I am Bull of Seven Fights / I am vulture on cliff / . . . I am word of skill. . . ." The Indo-European connection is most striking in the Bhagavad-Gita when Krishna declares, "I am the radiant sun among the light-givers / among the stars of night I am the moon / . . . I am the ocean among the waters . . . / I am the dice-play of the cunning / I am the silence of things secret." As Tolkien has remarked, the "intricately knotted and ramified history of the branches on the tree of tales is closely connected with the philologist's study of the tangled skein of language."

With the last settlement came an aristocratic society based on a cattle-raising economy. Law and legend and societal structure would survive into the historic period in Britain in feudal practices and customs. The deity/heroes have their counterparts in British legend and literature, like Maeve in Ireland who became Queen Mab of the fairies in England. They are with us still in folk tales and legends, and in children's books by George MacDonald and Rudyard Kipling and John Masefield and Edward Eager and Lloyd Alexander and Susan Cooper and Alan Garner and C. S. Lewis and William Mayne and P. L. Travers and Rosemary Sutcliff and Diana Wynne Jones and innumerable others, recently and notably Eloise McGraw.

More important, you will find ideas and narrative patterns repeated in endless variation in fiction containing no supernatural occurrences. Heroes and heroines journeying into the unknown because they must, seeking and finding. Real journeys may also be true in the mythic sense. Like the epic journeys of myth, the starting point is usually beyond any one person's control, beyond choice. It is dictated by governments or parents, by hunger or terror. Every time the balance of the world shifts, people stream forth like lemmings, like heroes.

In children's literature, stories about journeys that depart from the traditional model are neither better nor worse than hero tales. But when they bring to life an unlikely hero, they perform a vital service to readers trying to sort out the truth about real life. Some characters, like Jerry in Robert Cormier's *The Chocolate War*, resist the lemming surge. Others, like Creep in Jill Paton Walsh's *A Chance Child*, may be powerless to break away. In a culture obsessed with winning, books like these remind us that we must choose our heroes well and take care how we show the others, the lemmings.

When we divide the world between Us and Them, the good guys and the bad, the light and the dark, the kings and the pig-keepers, the polar bears and the lemmings, we follow a time-worn tradition that comes close to perpetrating a lie. Even when we introduce an element of martyrdom in our lemming representative, we may be setting our children on a road that leads to the righteous acceptance of inhumanity. The signposts along the way usually direct the child toward Us, the good guys. That is why I value especially books that give the reader pause. These are the books that modify the clear view toward lemming-land and that cast up obstacles in the path that leads to grandiose heroism. When their authors attend to the import of the heroic ethic, as Le Guin does, as Cooper does, as Alexander does when he reminds us that we are all assistant pig-keepers, hero tales can be wonderful.

So, too, can lemming tales that pattern either metaphoric or literal journeys. Like lemmings that burrow in the tundra, their characters may be invisible to many people.

When we consider the biological and social genesis of epic journeys and their heroes, when we look at the connection between the predator and the warrior, we do not diminish the stature of the great heroes of song and story or the stature of their journeys. Achilles and Cúchulain and Beowulf and Arthur transcend the sociobiological and historical accounting of human beings on the move. They spring from the imagination, and in them human endeavor and human limits are joined with superhuman ideals.

Lemming-sized heroes allow us to recognize the individual in the mass and to believe, always, that every life has possibility. The unwilling traveler in a children's book informs the young reader about such possibility, informs the heart as well as the mind. Such stories hint at the hero or polar bear in the lemming and at the lemming in the polar bear. When we find ourselves already launched on a journey whose end can or cannot be predicted, we discover that it matters how we go, even if we can't help going. Some choice is always with us, and even in the smallest way can make a difference.

Books with convincing unheroic heroes turn the idea of lemmings inside out. And after all, the idea of lemmings is no more true than the idea of polar bears. Lemmings are not martyrs, although they may suffer martyrdom.

Children who find a single important life in the ordinary, unimportant, and unheroic are less likely to succumb to the human fallacy of Us versus Them. They will be less likely to accept the notion that thousands of terrified refugees of war do not feel as we do, or that millions crammed into cattle cars on journeys they could not escape belong to a subhuman horde.

To give young readers a particular face, a voice, a human life to mourn and to rejoice in, is to protect them against the lie and to arm them with the truth—to help them discern the direction they are heading in their own life journey and to imagine the possibilities and responsibilities along the way.

These remarks were made at *Writing the World: Myth as Metaphor,* CLNE at Trinity College, Dublin, Ireland, in 1995.

HOMECOMING

TOM FEELINGS

The wise have said, "To know who you are is the beginning of wisdom."

For many years now when I'm asked who I am, I say that I am an African who was born in America. This answer connects me specifically with my past and present and gives me direction for all future work, because I believe I bring to my work a quality that is rooted in the culture of Africa and extended by the experience of being black in America.

For African Americans, struggle has been an unavoidable condition, and pain a constant companion.

To me, pain and joy are the two strongest opposing forces affecting our lives in America. As an artist, I have long subscribed to the dictum of Jean Toomer, a black writer, who said that "an artist is he who can balance strong contrast, who can combine opposing forms and forces in significant unity." For me, a significant part of our heritage in America—and a driving force in my own work—is that constant combining and balancing of seemingly unequal forces.

The key for me has been my concentration on the past, and

that is the reason I now live in America's Deep South, where so much of that history resides.

In his TV series *The African*, Ali Mazuri said this:

> Because of their ordeal as slaves in America, many black Americans lost the consciousness of being African. But the worst of it is that America tried to teach them to be ashamed of Africa. . . . And they had to carry a badge . . . not only of being ex-slaves . . . but of race. Most Americans have their names as a collective group, traced to their geographical origins, or to their cultural origins. . . . Jewish Americans, Italian Americans, Irish Americans . . . so on. . . . But when it comes to this special group, it became Negro or black. You stop referring to geography and culture; you are referring instead to race—to color.
>
> It means that the entire history of this country has one compelling lesson for the people of African ancestry: forget your ancestry—remember your skin color—forget you're African—remember you're black.
>
> Italian Americans, Irish Americans, Swedish Americans know what village their father or grandfather departed from to come to America. But for African Americans, it was different—they don't know which village . . . which community in Africa they sprang from. They have been denied the right to be homesick because they are not sure where their home is. They have been denied the privilege of nostalgia because their ancestors, enslaved, were uprooted rudely and blindly.

But Africa for me was my sanctuary. Living and traveling in Africa helped me to see that we have a special view of America and of the world because of the way we came to this country, because of our four centuries of going through the fires of hell. It is a view shared by no other group in America (with the exception of the Native Americans who have their own unique story to tell). Though our enslavement brought us pain, misery, debasement, and not surprisingly, degrees of self-hatred, we have improvised within this restricted environment. And survived.

The constant struggle for equality and the consistent denial of the status of first class citizens have forced us to see behind the brave slogans, the plastic flags, and the glitter of white America's majority. All those symbols of freedom Americans love to display to the rest of the world.

It is not enough to be smart, white, middle-class, and male.

Here is a statement from a magazine interview with former president Jimmy Carter:

> There is still an element of racism that is inherent in perhaps all of us. I try not to be a racist and wouldn't call myself a racist, but I have feelings that border on it. And that is embarrassing to me sometimes. When the TV screens were filled with little Ethiopian and Sudanese children walking along with distended bellies and dying in the arms of their dying mothers, it's hard for me to believe that one of these children, in the eyes of God, is as important as Amy, my daughter. How many of these little black kids does it take to equal one Amy? Fifteen? Twenty? Ten? Five? I think the answer is one. But it's hard for me to believe this. I think all of us to some degree are guilty of an insensitivity to the needs and ideas of others.

This is an honest man, publicly vomiting up a lot of the unpleasant pain from his training, his programming, his past, by admitting his own responsibility for it here in the present. It is not an easy thing to do. But he shows with humility that it can be done. The ability for human beings to mature, open up, take in new information and grow, is what makes us unique in this world.

Will we learn from our past? Are we doomed to repeat the same mistakes? Not if we begin telling all the children the truth about this huge house—this building we all live in, called the United States of America. Tell them about the climate, the atmosphere, the environment it was built on—who it was taken away from. Tell them about the true conditions those great documents of freedom were created under. Tell them the truth about the men who wrote them. Tell them all of it.

We can risk it. And the children can take it.

They have not learned how to avoid the truth—yet. If we tell them the whole truth about our past, the good and the bad, that will at least give them definite clues as to why we are still having the same problems today. Give them the moral strength now in the present so they can finally eliminate these problems in the future. Help the children to realize that a house is not a home— it is the people inside, living, working together co-operatively within the building, who make it a home.

For me, in the last twenty-six years, home became the place I chose to be. The place where the work took me. Wherever I could use these skills, this talent, to help develop and change that society so that it could benefit all of its citizens, nurturing a familiarity with the language of art. Through work and with people, feeding the need for myself and others to understand the life around us and the world we live in, strengthening my belief that human beings can change those things that are bad into things that are good.

Home is where the heart is. Picture this. While working on the artwork of *The Middle Passage,* in my mind's eye I can see how complex, how confusing it all had to be for runaway slaves. On their way north, all the fear, hatred, and pain rose up in them at the sight of *any* white person, who potentially could be an old or a new owner, an overseer or a slave catcher sent to hunt them down and bring them back. And then how that all miraculously slid away when the joy of realization hit them: That this white face in front of them was a Quaker or an Abolitionist, or any one of the hundreds of conductors along the way who gave a helping hand up on the train to the underground railroad, heading straight for freedom. How it must have verified, justified, and strengthened their deepest belief and hope in the basic goodness of human beings. Even in those terrible times. And thank heavens I can open my eyes, right here, now, and still see some of those same faces, in this time: people who sincerely believe that all men and women are created equal, and who by the actions of their lives—every day— prove it.

They prove that home is where the heart is. It is not a place, but a feeling.

These remarks were made at *Homecoming,* CLNE at Saint Michael's College, Colchester, Vermont, in 1990.

ILLUSTRATION REPRINTED WITH PERMISSION OF ATHENEUM BOOKS FOR YOUNG READERS, AN IMPRINT OF SIMON & SCHUSTER CHILDREN'S PUBLISHING DIVISION, FROM *THE WIND IN THE WILLOWS* BY KENNETH GRAHAME, ILLUSTRATED BY ERNEST H. SHEPARD. COPYRIGHT © 1933 CHARLES SCRIBNER'S SONS; COPYRIGHT © RENEWED 1961 BY ERNEST H. SHEPARD. LINE DRAWING BY E. H. SHEPARD COPYRIGHT UNDER THE BERNE CONVENTION, REPRODUCED BY PERMISSION OF CURTIS BROWN, LONDON.

DULCE DOMUM

JOHN ROWE TOWNSEND

"Home" is one of those words that hardly need to be defined. They are universal and familiar, the everyday building blocks of thought and expression. But if a simple definition is required, it might be that "home is the place where you feel you belong." This implies psychological as well as physical belonging. A person's home ground need not in these days be narrowly limited; it could be a city, a country, perhaps even a continent. Clive James, an Australian writer who is now a British TV personality, once said, "My homeland is the English language." But home may also, obviously, be somewhere small, individual, snug, private.

My starting point will be *The Wind in the Willows*. My text is "Dulce Domum," for which the rough translation is "home, sweet home." It's the heading for the chapter in which Mole, returning with Rat from a long day's outing in the country, feels a sudden electric thrill, a call from the void that makes him tingle through and through. It's the call of home, the little home that he had abandoned so unthinkingly the day he first found the river. The subject assigned to me is home as sanctuary, or place as sanctuary; the first meaning of the word *sanctuary* is "a holy place," and in this particular chapter of *The Wind in the Willows* one could

fairly attach that meaning; but a looser and more general meaning of sanctuary is a place of refuge, and elsewhere in *The Wind
in the Willows* we shall see home as a place of refuge and also home
as a place under attack, a fortress from which the enemy must be
driven out.

My first introduction to *The Wind in the Willows* took place at
school, in the local elementary school, many years ago, when I
was in the equivalent, I suppose, of about fourth grade. We had
a splendid teacher, a maiden lady of the old school, Miss Annie
Cox; and for the last half-hour on Friday afternoons she would
give us a weekly treat by reading to us, usually from a children's
classic. While she chose the books, we in the class had a certain
amount of say, in that she allowed us to accept or reject her
choices, a privilege of which we availed ourselves to the full.
None of us had ever actually read any of the books; we judged
them strictly by their titles. We gladly accepted *Treasure Island*
and *The Jungle Book*, but gave the thumbs-down to *Little Women*
and *A Little Princess*, which we had no doubt would be soppy
stuff. (I realize as I tell you this that it was the boys who were
most vociferous; maybe in those days little girls who had reached
the age of nine were conditioned to being the acquiescent sex.)

One week, after finishing the book she had just been reading,
Miss Cox offered us *The Wind in the Willows*. We groaned. That
didn't sound very exciting. No promise in *that* title of fighting and
bloodshed, which were what we really liked. Miss Cox accepted
our verdict and read something else; but a few weeks later she
proposed to us *The Adventures of Mr. Toad*. That seemed much more
promising. "Adventure" was always a good word. We approved
of adventure. We assented readily. And of course we were
hooked at once. We liked the Toad chapters best—what child
doesn't?—but the river-bank chapters and "The Wild Wood"
also held us without difficulty. Miss Cox read us all the book with
the reasonable exceptions of "The Piper at the Gates of Dawn"
and "Wayfarers All." I still remember the gasp that went round

the class when she revealed at the end that we had been listening to *The Wind in the Willows.*

I was so impressed that I saved up my pocket-money and bought a copy. It was the first book I ever bought for myself. My Aunt Madge, who was herself a teacher, took me to buy it, and with great percipience refrained from buying it for me as a gift. Admirably, I now think, she stood by while I counted out my own hard-earned, or at any rate hard-saved pennies. The book cost one shilling and sixpence—about thirty-five cents—and instantly became, *because* I had bought it myself, one of my most prized possessions. I have it still, a modest little brown-backed volume with much-thumbed pages and no pictures. I don't believe I ever made a better buy.

Home is a recurrent theme in *The Wind in the Willows;* you could almost say it's a book about homes. I don't think we get much description of Rat's home, although on page three, when Mole first catches sight of the hole in the riverbank that is its entrance, he immediately thinks what a nice snug dwelling-place it would make for an animal with few wants and fond of a bijou riverside residence. But actually Rat's home is the river itself. Mole's and Badger's and Toad's homes, however, are the settings of three key episodes.

For Kenneth Grahame himself the concept of home was crucial. He had, as he told a friend in a letter written when he was thirty-seven and still a bachelor, a recurrent dream of homecoming. It was of coming home to a little room, quietly tucked away somewhere and reached, if I remember correctly, up a lot of stairs—a room that was absolutely and totally *his,* holding his favorite books, his favorite chair, his favorite belongings, a room that welcomed him home and that for him was the ultimate safe place, the ultimate sanctuary.

This dream had so powerful a hold upon Kenneth Grahame that he toyed with the notion that his dream-room did exist somewhere in London, and that he had been there, but had unfortunately forgotten where it was. If he is to be believed, he actually looked for it in the back streets of Bloomsbury and Chelsea—two of the more bohemian districts of London—but, not surprisingly, he never found it. As he said,

> It waits, that sequestered chamber, it waits for the serene moment when the brain is in just the apt condition, and ready to switch on the other memory even as one switches on the electric light with a turn of the wrist. Fantasy?—well, perhaps. But the worst of it is, one can never feel quite sure. Only a dream, of course. And yet—the enchanting possibility!

Peter Green points out in his biography, *Kenneth Grahame*, published in 1959—a book to which I am much indebted—that at that time in his life, which was actually his most productive phase, Grahame was in urgent need of finding what he had never truly possessed, a place of his own. "His life since childhood had been rootless and transitory, never more than a year or two in any one place. There had been no real ties of domestic affection to bind him to any of them. The result of this was a psychological characteristic that recurs throughout his work: a strong but unanalyzed homing instinct towards an ideal home that had never in fact existed. This instinct acts as a counterbalance to Grahame's equally strong wanderlust: They maintain an uneasy balance of tension."

As a child, Grahame had been deprived of any real home. He was born in Scotland of solid bourgeois stock. His mother died when he was just five; his father couldn't or wouldn't look after the children and sent them to live with their maternal grandmother. In all his published work, Grahame never mentions either his mother or his father. The grandmother seems to have done her duty, but without enthusiasm; there were other relatives around and a fair amount of money but not much emotional warmth. Later, in *The Golden Age* and *Dream Days*, Grahame offered a disconcerting child's-eye view of the adult world, of those he called the Olympians; and the assumption is that his own relatives were the inspiration. He was sent to a private school at Oxford, and he expected to go to Oxford University, but here came his second deprivation. His Uncle John Grahame, who held the money-bags, was a hard-headed practical Scot who didn't feel inclined to pick up the tabs. In those days you couldn't go to Oxford unless you could pay, so that was that, and Uncle John got him a clerkship in the Bank of England.

I'll whiz through the rest of his career quickly. He rose through the Bank of England to become its secretary—a very senior post—before he was forty, but he doesn't seem to have exerted himself unduly, and his brother-in-law, Lord Courtauld-Thomson, remarked that "his duties as Secretary may have suggested the titles *Golden Age* and *Dream Days*." At about the same time as becoming Secretary of the Bank he married a lady called Elspeth Thomson; they seem not to have been well suited to each other, and his married life wasn't particularly happy. And he wrote practically nothing ever again, with the one great exception of *The Wind in the Willows*, nine years later in 1908. He then left the Bank—it's not clear whether he jumped or was pushed—and for the remaining twenty-four years of his life he didn't do anything much except sit at home or occasionally travel, living on what was now a comfortable income. He and Elspeth had one son, Alastair, who was born blind in one eye and with a squint in the other. Alastair had a hard time at school and university and was killed on a railroad track just before his twentieth birthday; it was almost certainly suicide, though the merciful inquest verdict was accidental death.

The Wind in the Willows is full of the tensions already mentioned. To begin with, Grahame, like his fellow Scot Robert Louis Stevenson, was brought up among Philistines who were

actually opposed to a literary career as being frivolous and effem-
inate. Stevenson reacted violently against this; he wrote full-
blooded fiction; lived, so far as his health allowed, a full-blooded
life; and died far away in the South Seas. But Grahame was only
half a rebel; he never really kicked over the traces. We may note
that at the very beginning of *The Wind in the Willows* Mole walks
out on his home and his settled way of life; but he doesn't actually go very far—only as far as the River Bank. He takes to heart
Rat's warning: The Wild Wood is a place to keep away from; and
beyond the Wild Wood comes the Wide World; and that, says
Rat, is "something that doesn't matter, either to you or me. I've
never been there, and I'm never going, nor you either, if you've
got any sense at all." And later Toad is firmly reproved by Badger for dashing around and getting into trouble rather than staying at home where he belongs and looking after Toad Hall.
Oddest of all, when Rat meets the Wayfaring Rat, gets the wanderlust, and says he's going south, Mole grapples with him and
literally holds him down until, in the words of the book, he is sane
again. Rebellion in fact is a powerful temptation, but the Grahame response to it is ultimately one of cautious withdrawal.

The principal episode in which a place, a home, is refuge is
when Mole ventures into the Wild Wood, disregarding Rat's
warning that this is the haunt of weasels, stoats, foxes, and others
that can't be trusted. Mole is terrified by the whistlings and pat-
terings and wicked little faces peering from holes; Rat comes to
rescue him, but the snow falls, they're lost and in trouble, and
then, providentially, Rat uncovers the front door of Mr. Badger.
And now they are safe; all is warmth and coziness and a good fire
and good companionship.

Dulce domum, home sweet home. It is both the most obvious
and the most profound of truisms that a child needs a home. But
it could be that in the age of the nuclear family, intensely turned
in upon itself rather than turned outward towards the extended
web of relationships that is now diminishingly likely to surround

it, parents have a special need not to hold their children too tightly for too long. The nuclear family, a unit of parents and dependent children under one roof, if it avoids breakup by death or divorce, must nevertheless break up sometime. When I was in mid-teens, I used to spend a lot of time at the home of a lively, argumentative Irish household consisting of two hospitable parents and five bright, friendly, intelligent children, the youngest about my age and the oldest in her early twenties. They were a natural center of gravity, and young people like myself from small families were inevitably attracted to their house. They themselves never went to anybody else's house; they didn't need to. I thought they were wonderful, a joy to be with; my mother was jealous of the hours and days I spent with them. Then time and fate took me away, and for about fifteen years I didn't see them. When I went back they were still there in the same house; none of them had married or looked likely to do so; the parents were now elderly and the children somewhat dispirited. They all doted on the dog. And it was plain for anyone now to see that they had been far too deeply embedded in the home. The fact is that children need to go away. As parents, we never, I hope and believe, perform our last service to our children until death cuts us off; but we have to perform a last act of actual child-rearing by letting our children go. Unless you go away, there can be no such thing as homecoming.

These remarks were made at *Homecoming*, CLNE at Saint Michael's College, Colchester, Vermont, in 1990.

THE HEROIC PERSONALITY

MADELEINE L'ENGLE

Picture a middle-aged man slumped in a wheel chair, unable to move, unable to speak except through a mechanical voice. It is difficult for him even to swallow his own saliva. And he is a hero, married to a heroine.

His name is Stephen Hawking, and he has amyotrophic lateral sclerosis, the same disease that killed Lou Gehrig. This disease usually kills in two or three years, but in Stephen Hawking it has moved unexpectedly and unusually slowly. After the diagnosis of the life-threatening disease, he fell apart; but then the disease did not progress and he met and married his wife, Jane, fathered three sons, and has become the most exciting physicist since Einstein. His wife has kept him in the world, preventing him from being isolated by his illness, traveling with him, giving dinner parties, refusing to let his disease deny him the stimulation and challenge of fellow human beings.

He is a hero because he has overcome fearful odds, because his mind is unfettered as it roves the universe, seeking for the Grand Unified Theory that will put together Einstein's theories of relativity with the discoveries of particle physics. He is a hero because he can still laugh, see the humor in life, and announce, "My goal is simple. It is a complete understanding of the universe, what it is and why it exists at all."

The heroic personality always has unusual odds to overcome, and ultimately enlarges our own understanding of the extraordinary universe in which we live. As Hawking says, "We see the universe the way it is because if it were different we would not be here to observe it." For our universe is made in such a way that it has taken a great number of seeming coincidences to produce a potential habitat for human life. For instance, if our gravity were even a fraction less than it is, all stars would be red dwarves and human life would be impossible; if it were a fraction greater, all stars would be blue giants and human life would be equally impossible.

So, in a sense, Creation has done the heroically impossible in giving us a universe which is capable of producing strong young suns with planetary systems, and an atmosphere that is precisely right for the arrival of human beings who grow, question, wonder, search, tell stories.

I had a lot of heroes and heroines when I was a child, and I believe that heroes are essential for our own development, because they are models for us, giving us hope that we, too, can do amazing things, beyond ordinary capacity. I still need heroic people to look up to in order to live my own life creatively.

My favorite heroine when I was nine or ten years old was Emily of New Moon. Emily was the creation of L. M. Montgomery, better known for her *Anne of Green Gables* series. I liked Anne, and still do, but Emily was special to me. Emily's father was dying from diseased lungs; my father was dying from lungs that had been mustard gassed in the war that was supposed to end war, but that started a century of war. Emily had some rather frightful and manipulative uncles and aunts who might have smothered her Emilyness if she had not stubbornly resisted. Emily helped me keep my own Madeleineness. Emily wanted to be a writer, and so did I. Emily was ecstatic over the beauties of this planet, and though I lived in a very different geography, Manhattan Island being nothing like Prince Edward Island, I, too, could move from grief to joy at the sight of a tiny new moon curled around a star. Emily understood that there is more to the world than the limited realm of provable fact; she had a touch of what the Scots called Second Sight, a fearful gift that occasionally brushed by me. Emily gave me the courage and the will to go on writing my stories and poems when my middle-grade teachers thought me stupid and worthless. It is not easy to retain a sense of validity when one is denigrated by peers and teachers alike. I needed Emily.

And since I was a totally unsuccessful schoolchild, I needed other heroes and heroines to give me some kind of a sense of value. I would come home from school, go into my own little back bedroom in my parents' apartment in New York, and gratefully move into the real world of story. I learned from George MacDonald's Curdie, from the princess, from the wise old woman who lived at the top of a flight of stairs that was not always there; these people were totally real for me. When Curdie had to plunge his hands into that extraordinary fire of roses, I felt the burning in my own hands. After that purifying, Curdie could always tell, when shaking someone's hand, what that person was really like. A hand might feel like a snake, or a hawk's talon, or the trusting hand of a child. And a handshake has never again been merely a handshake for me.

I read the Greek and Roman myths, the *Iliad* and the *Odyssey*, but I liked even better E. Nesbit's fantasies and her stories of the Bastable children. I needed people I could identify with, rather than the superheroes of the Greeks and Romans. And one of my favorite heroines was Mary Lennox of Frances Hodgson Burnett's *The Secret Garden*. Now, on the surface,

Mary does not seem to embody many heroic qualities. She is nasty and self-centered and spoiled. But she has a strong sense of survival, holding on to her own identity as she leaves India, where her parents are both dead of cholera, to go to Yorkshire to stay with a crotchety uncle. The discovery of the secret garden, and the turning of it into a thing of beauty, is as much the discovery of Mary's heart as it is of the physical garden. And I thought, if Mary can come through all this, and grow, and learn to love, then maybe so can I. And perhaps the most important thing I learned was that a person who has heroic qualities is *human*, and does not have to be perfect.

I teach a class in techniques of fiction at a school on the upper west side of New York City. The class is a wonderfully mixed bag of kids, Caucasian, Asian, black, and they are there because they want to be, not because they have to be. One week I asked them to write a character sketch of someone they admired. In the class that year there was a brilliant black girl, legitimately angry about many things, but also loving. And when she handed me her paper, she had written, "I'm sorry, I've really tried, but I can't think of anybody I admire."

The other students were as upset by this as I was, and kept offering her suggestions: "Mother Theresa of Calcutta? Martin Luther King? John F. Kennedy? Madame Curie?" But she kept shaking her head.

I didn't realize then what I do now, that she felt that an admirable or heroic person has to be perfect. She is not the only one to suffer from this illusion. It is, in fact, foisted on us by society. We know, to our rue, that those we admire are not perfect, and because they are not perfect, the tendency is to demolish them. When a strong public figure dies, almost immediately biographies appear to show that whoever it was wasn't very good after all, he had mistresses, she took drugs, they weren't really any better than the rest of us, so let's wipe them out.

But that's one of the most important things about the heroic character. Mary Lennox, Hazel (the rabbit in *Watership Down*), Cat Chant in Diana Wynne Jones's *Charmed Life*, are not any better than the rest of us, and that is why they give us hope. If Remi, the orphan boy of Hector Malot's *Nobody's Boy*, can hang in there through terrible tragedies and adventures, then so can we. The heroic characters who give me hope and courage are not impossible ideals with qualities of bravery and strength I can never attain to, but ordinary people who somehow or other manage to do extraordinary things.

When did we start being told that our heroic characters had to be perfect or they couldn't be heroic? I'm not sure, but I think it was not too many decades ago, when the media started calling all of us consumers. What a dehumanizing epithet! Why did we ever allow the media to talk us into thinking of ourselves as consumers? What is a consumer? A forest fire consumes. Cancer consumes. AIDS consumes. Anton Chekhov, John Keats, and Emily Brontë died of T.B., which used to be called consumption, because it consumed its victims.

The heroic personality cannot be a consumer. And I suspect that not one of us here wants to be a consumer, either. Consumerism is death, and the heroic character leads us to life. We human beings are called to be human, to be nourishers, givers, lovers, not consumers. A consumer is only expected to buy more and more.

The heroic personality is human, not perfect, but human. Perfectionism, like consumerism, is one of the great cripplers. If I have to do something perfectly I'll probably not do it at all, in case I fail. Maybe it's a good thing I was such a failure as a schoolchild, because accepting failure has freed me to take risks. Marriage is a terrible risk, so is friendship, or having children, or writing a book. If I had to be perfect I'd never sit at the piano and struggle to play a Bach fugue or a Mozart sonata, and I'd miss a lot of joy.

And to be human is to be fallible. I don't know about you,

but what I learn from is my mistakes, not the things I do right, but my mistakes. It is fine to be fallible!

When I was a child I used to think that being grown-up meant that we would know everything. Grown-ups had the answers. This is an illusion that a lot of people don't lose when they grow up. But our very fallibility is one of our human glories, and what makes it possible for us occasionally to be heroic. And even the great heroes make appalling mistakes— Odysseus, Charlemagne, Bonny Prince Charlie.

There are some creatures who are not given the blessing of fallibility, those insects who live totally by instinct—and their instincts have to be infallible, or they are dead. Every ant in an ant colony knows exactly what to do and when to do it and where to do it and how to do it, and an ant who deviates from the infallible instinctual pattern is a goner. An ant has superb instincts, but precious little free will. And free will is an essential element of a story. Are there any good stories written with an ant as the protagonist? I can't think of any. Wart, the young King Arthur of *The Once and Future King,* learns a lot about the horrors of infallibility when Merlin sends him to the ant world where everything that is not forbidden is compulsory. There are lots of stories about mice, or rabbits, and one of my all-time favorites is Kenneth Grahame's *The Wind in the Willows* with the wonderfully anthropomorphic characters, Mole, and Rat, and Badger, and Toad. Free will involves fallibility. Like our favorite fictional characters we try something new. We make mistakes. We learn from them. We try something else, and maybe that doesn't work, so we try something else again.

Perfection and moral virtue have not always been combined. I looked *perfect* up in one of my etymological dictionaries and found that the word *perfect* comes from the Latin and means "to do thoroughly." So perhaps we need to redefine perfect. If it really means "to do thoroughly," then one might say that it means to be human, to be perfectly and thoroughly human, and that is what is meant by being perfect: human, not infallible or impeccable or faultless, but human.

So I do want my protagonists to be perfect, defining perfect as thorough, thoroughly human, making mistakes, sometimes doing terrible things through wrong choices, but ultimately stretching themselves beyond their limitations. When I read for pleasure—and I believe that reading for pleasure is a very important exercise—I want to be challenged, given hope, and sometimes strength I didn't know I had. I don't enjoy reading books about discontented women who end up even more discontented than they started, and I don't like reading books about anti-heroes. This is not reading for pleasure! When I go to a bookstore I head for three departments—young adult novels, mysteries, and fantasy and science fiction, because in these books I am most likely to find protagonists I can identify with and care about, and who embody for me the heroic ideal.

In the Middle Ages in Britain the local dukes and earls used to put on their armor and go out and fight each other, mostly for no particular reason. It was what dukes and earls who had armor did. In the evening there would be a banquet, and then the *schopp*, who was a predecessor of the minstrel, would sing the day's battle for the people, telling them what had happened, giving it shape and pattern. So, from time immemorial, the singer, the poet, the story-teller gave meaning to what might otherwise be merely chaos. Leonard Bernstein said that for him, music is cosmos out of chaos. And so is story, for us human beings who understand ourselves largely through the telling of our stories.

We all know that story is work—glorious, exciting work, but work. It means using our incredible gift of free will as our protagonists are faced with choices—and making a choice is always an important part of a story. And it means opening ourselves to new ideas, to surprises—for the reader as well as the writer. What a surprise to discover that Luke is Loki, or that Sara Crewe can make friends with a rat, or that a rooster and a dog and a dun cow can make me weep.

Perhaps Stephen Hawking is a hero for me because he is trying to tell the story of the entire universe, why it is here at all, how it began, what it means. When he was asked how his illness had affected his work, he replied that it had freed him to do nothing but think. And his thinking is opening up the glories of the universe as he struggles to tell the story. He knows that he is not infallible. His body is anything but perfect. But he is a nourisher, not a consumer, and he is a story-teller and a hero and I am grateful, because I need heroes and heroines, in life and in literature.

Thank heavens for the princess who feels the pea of injustice under all those mattresses of indifference; and those other two (or are they really one) princesses, one of whom speaks pieces of gold, and the other toads and snakes—we all have our toad days, and more rarely the gold ones. And thanks, too, for the dragon-slayers, and even for the dragons themselves. And thank heavens for all of you who care about story and who are heroes and heroines yourselves.

These remarks were made at *The Heroic Ideal: Legacy and Promise*, CLNE at the Massachusetts Institute of Technology, Cambridge, Massachusetts, in 1988.

TAKE YOUR TIME

VIRGINIA HAMILTON

I am a product of Midwest America. The mighty Ohio River, some sixty miles from my home, forms great loops in my imagination as it does actually on its snake-and-wind through rich borderland. Time, in such rural places of America, moves slower than in other, larger places. No huge shopping mall has descended upon the populace overnight, forever changing the rural landscape. No McDonald's or Burger King to mar the rural north entrance into the village. The one Kentucky Fried Chicken franchise, located to the south out of town and on the highway to Xenia, the county seat, took years to pass stringent rules of the zoning, planning, and priority boards.

My mother, now ninety-six years old, was born in Yellow Springs. Her father came there as a fugitive from injustice. The story of Grandpa Perry's journey from the slave state of Virginia to Ohio defines the parameters of my creative writing. That I am named Virginia can be no accident. I am the only one of generations named for a state. Serendipity. If I have the aptitude for making desirable discoveries by accident, and I do, time and time again, so too did my mother, at least once. By naming me Virginia she made me ever aware of my legacy and my responsibility to history as it relates to my historical past. Ancestry. I am of two minds within my writing, to say nothing of the female force of gender.

I begin a book with a character. I find I write against that character. There is often the stability of tradition and traditional life—timelessness—which is the character's background in opposition with the transient and unstable modern urban life—and time—usually represented by another more worldly character. The power of these opposites is dealt with in separate ideas—past and present, light and dark, staying and leaving, natural and supernatural, tradition, superstition, and enlightenment. Somewhere between the opposites is a synthesis or balance.

My characters have contradictory desires, as do I. Tradition and at least the slowing down of time is likely to win out in my books, but with a profound feeling of sadness and loss.

My being part of a parallel culture—of a minority group in a sense in opposition spiritually and societally to the empowered American culture—adds, I think, to this sense of opposition in my characters. They want to be American; they are black. They are uncertain of their position in society. They move through life and time with dis-ease. They seek some relief from the conflict. They know that any moment of time and in any place the American dream can become a bad dream and may well become their nightmare. This then is their reality. My grandfather fled slavery toward freedom. But did he find it? My characters search for happiness; does this search cause them to move, to run?

Time is of quality. Remember the time? A grand time was had by all. Once upon a time. In the beginning. My time is your time. Time to leave. Time to be born. Time to live. Time to die. There is no time.

Time is of quantity. I spent all day. Time hangs heavily. I have time on my hands. His shoulders were bent, were weighted by time. She let time dribble away.

What does happen to time in a book? Whose time is there in a book? What happens to the writer's time; what is its significance, its definition? In a fiction, several kinds of time seem to be at work simultaneously. The real time of the author ceases to exist as she becomes immersed in the time and place of a fiction or nonfiction and within the intensity and time-beat of characters. What begins then is the time of the novel, and the march in time of characters, within which time expands and contracts as if it were a living entity.

In my most experimental work, titled *Arilla Sun Down,* I use all manner of literary devices to expand, bend, and contract time. My main idea for the book was my observation that we all carry our pasts around with us. Some of that past is conscious, but a good deal of it remains steeped in childhood or the layers of the unconscious. Nevertheless, we respond to that past as though we remembered it, through mannerisms, tone of voice. We reflect the looks of mothers, grandparents, and so forth. We have character propensities that sometimes are unfathomable to us, but may seem perfectly reasonable to a relative who observes biological evolution in action. "Son, you walk just like your granddaddy. You never knew him, but you walk and sound just like him," a relative might say.

My thought was to give the past and present in *Arilla Sun Down* a feeling of simultaneousness by alternating different time frames and focusing as though both were there in the present before the reader's eyes. The protagonist is a teenager but the book opens when she is a small child. The language of the narration is stylized to reflect the distortion in time and the otherworldliness of unknown memory. The child would not remember her early years. So the author uses poetic license.

From chapter one, page one of *Arilla Sun Down:*

> Late in the big night and snow has no end. Taking me a long kind of time going to the hill. Would be afraid if not for the moon and knowing Sun-Stone Father is sledding. Way off, hear him go, "Whoop-eeeee!" Real thin sound, go "Whoop-eeeee!"
>
> If Mother could see me, she would say, *What*

you doing up? Get back under the covers. Catching your
death. But Mama sleeping on. I can slip on out to the
moondust snow. She not seeing everything I do, like
she say.

  Now hurry to follow all of the tracks going deep
in the snow. Knowing there is some big hill where
all tracks of children go. Downhill is deep in a
moonshade and ends at a cliff. Only Stone Father
can stop a sled in time. I can't stop it. Jack Sun Run
wouldn't care to try. I am smallest, knowing nothing
for sure. But I think my brother, Jack, is a horse.

  Jack Sun Run still sleeping. He is bigger. But I
am who slipping away.

Arilla finds her father and persuades him to sled with her
down the dangerous hill at the bottom of which there is no fence,
only a deep gorge. Her father tells her:

> "Arilla, now hear me. . . . If the creeps come over
> you, don't let loose, or I'll never catch you in the pre-
> sent time."
>
>   "Knowing that for sure," I saying. Downhill ends
> at a cliff. Over the cliff is another time. Having seen
> no one go over or coming back. They say three peo-
> ple have gone. Two boys and an uncle, so they say.

In Arilla's and her father's lifetime cycles, death is not the end
of time, but simply not the present time. It is described as "another
time," all things in their circle of life being equal.

  By the second chapter, we are back into what can be thought
of as a present time. Arilla is no longer a child. But let her speak
and you will see how she sounds in her present.

  For sure, my Birthday would be a disaster. I mean,

worse than the time they tell about when that Lear-
jet piloted by some rock-and-roll star-boys crash-
landed in Wilson Onderdock's Black-Angus
pasture a mile outside of town. Knowing something
about Black Angus and Onderdocks gives a clue to
what kind of engagement went on in that cow pasture for half the night. Even if one of the star-boys
was bleeding all over the place, Wilson Onderdock
said *nobody* was getting any blood transfusion and
an ambulance ride until his prize bull hanging in little chunks on the fence was paid for.

My Birthday was shaping up to be the same
kind of for-real bust. I would be surprised if there
wasn't a little blood and guts somewhere in it, too.
Because any event that had me at the edge of it
when I was supposed to be dead center, and had
Jack Sun Run at the center when he shouldn't've
been there at all, was doomed any sixteen ways you
wanted to look at it. It was just that with my
brother being the Sun, if the day didn't naturally
revolve around him, then it couldn't happen.

The power of the sun. We reckon time by the earth's rotation
around the sun, and so, too, do Arilla and the whole book, actually,
revolve through the time of this fictional world around Jack Sun
Run Adams. Between the time of the child, the first section that I
quoted from *Arilla Sun Down,* and the section about Arilla grown to
teenhood, lies time and its passage, change over years, parts of
which Arilla may actually recall. But she cannot recall all of it. A
gentle Indian man by the name of James False Face whose secret
name is Talking Story has profound influence over her development; so that, by the end of the book, when he, through a shadowy,
ghost, or dead time—he, himself is dead—reveals to Arilla her secret
name, she is already aware of it, and knows she is the Wordkeeper.

Wordkeeper?

"Hearing you, too."

Think of a time, any time, and I will be with you.

"But you going now?"

Yes.

"Can't I going with you?"

Yes, if you want to.

"Is it far—going?"

It is only going in a circle.

"Then you coming back again?"

I am here and now, then and there, in all things.

"You just going around."

Yes.

"Then I thinking to stay here."

Stay, then. Live with honor. And Wordkeeper?

"I hear you."

Remember who you are.

Time as a circle is an ancient concept. Think of Cronos devouring his own children, the offspring of time itself. It is also an Amerindian concept and that of countless other peoples. Ashes to ashes and dust to dust.

Because of the stylized language of this section, the psychic distance is not distracting. In fact, the psychic distance between the characters and the reader is almost nil. The reader feels that she or he is somewhere there between Wordkeeper and Talking Story, who is himself speaking softly either in Arilla Wordkeeper's head or in her ear. Stylization and a close-up psychic distance enables the author to avoid sentimentalizing Arilla's profound sense of loss of James False Face's death. We can use all manner of distancing to present events in time. "It was Saturday, Arilla Adams stood waiting." (That's one distance, rather remote and somewhat formal.) "Arilla hated being on a horse." (That's a closer distance.) "Lord, the smell of the horse made her ill." (Still closer.) "The rain seeped down her neck, it covered her hair, freezing, turning her lips blue." (Very close, indeed, we're right up front.) Psychic distancings are moves of a camera. Books usually begin with remote or medium shots; and as we focus in on the protagonist, we are close up and intimate or personal. The mind created the camera and as we see our characters in action, in time, place, and space, we see in terms of the camera eye.

I would guess that I am intimately involved in this Wordkeeper section I've quoted. The symbolism is great here. James False Face is a veiled reference to the James Weldon Johnson poem, "We Wear the Mask."

> We wear the mask that grins and lies
> It hides our cheeks and shades our eyes
> With torn and bleeding hearts we smile . . .
> We wear the mask!

James is also my father's middle name. It is certainly true that the exchange between Wordkeeper and Talking Story is somehow a farewell to my deceased father. It is I, the author, saying, "Never fear, what you desired all your life for yourself and was thwarted will be carried on by your children. There is a keeper and the keeper protects the flame through her time, and passes it along."

A version of "Take Your Time" appeared in *Travelers in Time: Past, Present, and to Come*, published in 1990 by Green Bay Publications,  Cambridge, England, in collaboration with Children's Literature New England. These remarks were made at *Travelers in Time: Past, Present, and to Come*, CLNE at Cambridge University, Cambridge, England, in 1989.

Illustration Copyright © Hal Siegal

TEMPLATES

JILL PATON WALSH

During the last year I have, for reasons I won't bore you with, changed the word-processing program that is my daily companion. The new one comes packaged with things called templates. You can choose templates for fax cover sheets, manuscripts, invoices, brochures, letters, theses, final demands, just about anything you could think of. You open a template and start to type; silently and invisibly the template formats what you are writing, sets margins, columns, fonts, headings, styles. . . . The ghostly presence of another hand and eye breathes o'er the page, shaping what you are doing. It is true that one can always override it, and I often do. But—and here's an odd thing—a decision to override the template doesn't feel the same as a decision to work entirely without one—on a pad of unmarked paper, for example.

None of the templates in the packages is marked "Story" or "Myth" or even "Folk tale"; and yet, surely, nobody since God on the first morning has been able to write on blank paper—the invisible template is always there. Of course, I can tell you a story. I can write one onto my template. I can't really write a myth—a myth isn't the sort of thing you write, you get given it with the rations, or you find it lying around secondhand in the great landfill site of culture. And without wanting to play the enticing game of definition chopping so often involved in using the word *myth*, I am prepared to say emphatically that if I write it myself it isn't a myth. For surely it is an essential part of the idea of myth that mythological stories once attracted a certain kind of belief, or still do attract a certain kind of belief, and it is not a kind of belief that we give to new stories, however true we may find them to be.

Could I write you a legend? Not really. Fundamentally a legend is *legenda*—that which ought to be read; we attach the word to narratives that are in the tradition, and liable to be knowledge expected of you—if you don't know the stories, you won't get the quotes.

"Is this the face that launched a thousand ships?"

"When you set out for Ithaca, ask that the voyage be long. . . ."

"A Trojan horse . . ."

"The Animals went in two by two. . . ."

I can't really write you a folk tale, either; I am not a folk. I am not even sure that you are folk within the meaning of the word, coming from far as you do, and multiple as you are, each one of you aware of more than one mythological tradition, and feasted on a plethora of millions of stories, old and new.

The best I could do with any of these kinds of narratives is retell them—they can never be told again, only retold.

I'd like to take a minute to consider the transformative impact of retelling on these different kinds of story. If you retell a myth when belief in it has vanished away—if you tell, for example, how fire was brought down to earth for the comfort of humans by a disobedient god called Prometheus, the result is not a myth. Your retelling may be a helpful contribution to *legenda*—the sort of thing one ought to know about in order to get the quotes. Remember Othello, contemplating murdering his wife:

> . . . But once put out thy light,
> Thou cunningest pattern of excelling nature
> And tell me where is that Promethean fire
> That can thy light relume?

Retelling myth-as-legend, and retelling legend too, is a generally helpful thing to do—brushing up the stories, refurbishing any fusty language, enticing a new generation of readers to swallow them happily, and become the kind of people who get the quotes, is a modestly useful activity. It is often done very nicely and lovingly, and published with glorious illustration. And it is nearly always done for children, for it is in childhood that it is felt to be needed—grown-ups are supposed to have done their homework already.

Retelling myth where a matrix of belief persists, as in doing stories from the Bible, for example, is a different thing, because it asks for a different reaction from hearers and readers. It asks for belief—in our days asks more often than it receives.

I would like to point out to you that to be any use at all this kind of retelling must be pretty faithful. To be told in childhood a story of the Trojan war in which the Greeks are defeated; to be told a tale in which King Arthur sits at a square table; to be told that a giraffe tempted Adam, and he ate the apple and gave a bit of it to Eve, would be to be seriously misinformed. Of course, there are spoof retellings that rely on the reader having heard the straight version first. Not so much retellings, as untellings, or counter-tellings. More about those anon.

For the moment I would like to muse with you about those templates. Let's look at an imaginary template called "Folk tale." What would be on it? A strong disposition towards a certain kind of gritty, circumstantial, and very traditional language, full of ritual phrases, like *once upon a time* and *happily ever after.* What else would be on it? If you accept the analysis offered by Bruno Bettelheim, you would find the template full of psychic drama. But I am not convinced by psychoanalysis; as a creative and female person I have always been very hard put to it to see the springs of art as sublimated envy for female procreative powers, and that has put me off Freud as an unchallengeable authority.

However, there is no doubt at all that folk tales have a force and an emotional power that is very difficult to account for if we look just at the surface story. Better than Bettelheim, to my way of thinking, is Derek Brewer, who describes folk tales as "a collection of symbolic stories." What are they symbolic of? They symbolize a family drama in which male protagonists must escape from the father figures, and find their fortunes, and their partners in life in a world outside the family; female protagonists must escape the custody of mothers, and allow the prince to find them, or if stuck with beasts and frogs must find transforming powers. According to Brewer's impressive analysis, the folk tale protagonists are three: father, mother, child. But there are numerous "splits": mothers, stepmothers, godmothers; fathers, ogres, giants; brothers and sisters and stepsisters. In a tale with three brothers the three are splits for the protagonist. Their cautions adumbrate different possible things for the protagonist to do, and identify the right one. The family drama plays out symbolically the conflict between love, hate, dependency, rebellion, following the protagonists through childhood difficulty to independent adult life with a partner of his or her own generation, a transition that has always been difficult, always haunted by fears and forbidden desires, and which remains so, substantially unchanged in our radically changed world. Folk tales are full of the consolations of luck, which are far from out of fashion, as queues to buy lottery tickets make clear. Luck both exonerates us from personal responsibilities for our miseries and indignities in life—it's our bad luck—and offers a welling source of hope—luck can change. Merit or rank are the bywords of the mighty and the gifted in the world, and luck the byword of the lowly.

Folk tales are often fairy tales, containing strictly impossible events (involving magic) and strictly nonexistent persons (like fairies), but they are not always impossible in this way. However, they nearly always seem preposterous considered as realism, and one of the reasons is neither psychological nor symbolic, but historical. Folk tales preserve, to an astonishing degree, the vanished circumstances of the past. The number of stepmothers in the canonical tales has often been remarked upon, and attributed rightly to the large number of second marriages in past societies in which the contribution of a wife to family economy was essential to survival, and childbirth was very dangerous and frequent, and often fatal. Our own age has restored stepmothers to relevance, through the prevalence of divorce and remarriage. And the situation of such families is no easier than it was, as far as one can tell. It is still a terrible strain to give the required filial affection and obedience to a parent figure who, not being a blood parent, does not necessarily have the instinctive attachment to the interests of the child. The father is often weak—in effect powerless to protect his children from his new wife. Why, incidentally, aren't there any folk tales about wicked stepchildren? We'll come to that later.

Stories about changelings are likewise full of a vanished historicity. Only too often communities in the past could not possibly afford to raise defective children. The tale that the child was a fairy child, a changeling, and that if you made it suffer enough, gave it no name, and starved it, the fairies would eventually take pity on their own offspring and take it back, is a very clear if brutal excuse for doing what had to be done in such cases. For the moment, let's look at something else, fairly closely related to changeling stories, which is part of the canonical body of folk tale, and which seems so preposterous that it is not read as realism, and that is the abandonment of children. I have been thinking a lot about it recently, because a feral child figures in *Knowledge of Angels.* This is a very old theme indeed. Oedipus, in the Theban stories, has been abandoned as a babe, exposed to die on the mountainside, because it has been prophesied that he will murder his father and marry his mother. The result is, you recall, that because he has no idea who his parents are he does just this; the taboos don't operate because of his ignorance. And sure enough, in the days when children were abandoned as a routine thing, it was the risk of inadvertent incest which most exercised the Church. Questions about whether it was lawful to enslave a babe who might have been born free also caused some agitation. Questions about abrogating parental duty, or about cruelty to the child concerned, hardly raised a ripple.

When was this? you will probably want to know. For to us, the stories about children found and raised by strangers seem quite as preposterous as the magic talismans, the helpful army of ants, and suchlike. They have a "folk tale" flavor; that is, the theme is symbolic of both fear and desire. We have all, when children wholly dependent for food and warmth upon an omnipotent adult, feared abandonment; we have probably likewise all longed to be the children of other parents, to be, were the truth known, sons and daughters of kings and queens, of rich and powerful people, whose bloodlines confer unearned dignity, and whose patronage is worth something. These desired secret parents would appreciate us, understand us, promote us. So strong a chord do the stories strike that we are almost compelled to read them symbolically. Both the story about the special child reared by commonplace parents and suddenly revealed in his or her true worth, and the story about a commonplace child earning a share of the inheritance—marrying the princess, taking a portion of the kingdom—are deeply satisfying to us as symbolic of our own internal story-telling about ourselves.

Yet it might seem just as reasonable to read adoption stories as realism. By realism I mean recognizable reflections of the external world. After all, it isn't difficult to think of a reason why Pharaoh's daughter might say she had found the baby in a basket in the bulrushes. And similarly, it isn't difficult to think of a reason why a woman might put her baby in a basket in the bulrushes just where Pharaoh's daughter would be likely to find him.

Moses in the bulrushes is a crucial example because it is both kinds of symbolic story, and it is a realistic story. It is an adoption story, in which the protagonist will side with his natural parentage—the Hebrews—against his adoptive parents—the Pharaohs. It is a hero story, in which the mysterious birth of the protagonist is a very familiar motif, and it is also something that might have happened. The abandonment of children to be brought up by strangers was something that happened in the past, not just very unusually but routinely. We have already touched on two examples from the ancient world; from late antiquity until the establishment of charitable orphanages in the eighteenth century the practice was normal. A family who could not rear a child would leave it somewhere public, usually the church steps, with a little salt to show it had been baptized, if it had been baptized, and sometimes tokens that, while not giving the game away immediately, might enable the natural parents to reclaim it later. A better-off family might pick up the baby and rear it, probably as a servant, though occasionally as a child of the new family. The food and clothing was usually worth investing, in a world in which muscle power was the only power available. Boys would become able to hew and carry, girls to weave and spin. If natural parents later reclaimed their offspring they had to repay the cost of nurture.

Do you remember the tangled plot of Mozart's *The Marriage of Figaro*? Figaro is being pursued by Marcellina; a bad case of unrequited love. What saves him is the sudden discovery that she is his mother. He doesn't know who his mother is, he tells the Count; he was found on a doorstep. His would-be bride recognizes the signs found with him. The audience laughs—what a turn up for the books! Marcellina gets her longed-for embrace from Figaro, and Figaro gets a slap from an outraged Suzanna, his sweetheart. Everyone puts her right—it's his mother. His mother? His *mother!* Oh, so that's all right then. The modern audience laughs uneasily; the overlap between lovers of opera and lovers of knock-about farce is not great. But Mozart's opera and the Beaumarchais play on which it was based were written in a century when as many as one in four children were abandoned in many French, Italian, and Spanish cities. There were certainly foster children of that kind in the audience for *The Marriage of Figaro*. The narrow avoidance of that dreaded incest risk would certainly have had poignancy for them, and no doubt they laughed heartily. John Boswell's book, *The Kindness of Strangers*, from which I am getting these facts, actually comments on how ironic it is that the substantial easing of the burdens of parenthood in modern times have rendered implausible, fanciful seeming, the bleak realities of the until-recent past.

We have run slap up against a problem in perception here: Our sense of what might really have happened is a highly modern one. In the light of John Boswell's book, we may well decide to reconsider the story of Figaro, and accept that this, which would be more or less impossible now, was possible then; but about magic, like women transformed into swans, or frog coachmen, we are resolute that such things could not have happened even then. If they could not have happened even then why do we not dismiss them out of hand? Because they speak to us so powerfully, figuratively. We do not mind the impossibilities because of the impressive veracity of the emotional pattern contained in the tale. We are all, or all have been, splits of the protagonist. The protagonist of folk tale is always, and intensely, a young person moving through ordeals into adult life. When adult state and a suitable partner is achieved the tale is over. Adults as such are of no interest—they exist only as helpers, enemies, or rivals of the protagonist. And this is why there are no wicked stepchildren in the tales. Stepmothers' feelings and problems are of no account—they are grown-ups and can work it out for themselves. They are fairly comprehensively warned that if they mistreat their fosterlings the tables may be turned later, and the warning is all the tale has to offer them.

For many centuries, and until very recent times, the craft of authorship was a craft of retelling. The most revered and loved authors were those who most skillfully rendered second- and third- and multi-hand stories, those whose tellings were so superlative as to be definitive. There could be more than one definitive version—the versions just accumulated. Think of the Fall of Troy; Homer's account occupied in ancient Greece a position rather like that of the Bible in medieval Europe. But Virgil turned it upside down. His version sides with the defeated Trojans, connects the escaping Aeneas to the foundation of Rome, and implicitly represents the Roman conquest of Greece as justified revenge. This doesn't go very well with Romulus and Remus, incidentally another abandoned child (or children) story, but Virgil fudges it. In the Middle Ages nobody is interested in the politics of the story, only in the personal fate of interesting individuals; the star-crossed lovers, Troilus and Cressida, emerge center stage. The horror of having an unchaste woman as the desired prize of armed conflict—an idea grossly removed from the ethics of knights and chaste fair ladies in the stories of the time—produces a chimerical Helen actually having it off with Paris within the walls of Troy, while the true Helen sits it out virtuously in Egypt. Cressida, a kind of split of Helen, carries the burden of shame, betraying Troilus, and giving rise to new versions embodying the bitterness of the betrayed lover, in Henryson's *Troilus and Cressida*, and in Shakespeare, though for once the bard's humanity is excelled by someone else's—for Chaucer's version is full of tenderness and understanding for Cressida.

The way we read now, with strict attention to the "drift" of a telling, with attention to the psychology of the personalities of the protagonists, there is no way in which all these versions of the war of Troy are the same story. But in the older mode of story-telling, protagonists didn't have personalities, they just had situations. And all these situations are drawn from a bucket marked "Troy." The craft of authorship was one of retelling; it was profoundly and organically connected with "authority" in the sense in which we now use it when we call someone an authority on DNA, or Roman political history, or the archaeology of—why not—Troy.

But sometime around two hundred and fifty years ago, there happened a profound cultural change, which faced authors with an entirely new demand—that they should be novel. That they should tell a new story, one never told before. That they should write novels. Novels are, by definition, new, and originally they were always realistic; that is, they offered a recognizable picture of the external and actual world. Whereas retellings are praised for faithfulness, or for superlative execution, novels are praised for originality. Originality as a virtue has been greatly reinforced by the copyright acts, which have turned retelling from the very heart of the art to a possible cause for a lawsuit, and there is no doubt that the merit of originality can be overstated.

"Bear in mind," my Oxford tutor said to me, "that new remarks about Shakespeare are wrong."

In view of the widespread impression that the novel is some kind of superlative fruit of an evolutionary tree, and vastly superior to precedent forms of prose story-telling, it is worth considering for a moment the effect of a sudden taste for originality on both author and audience. A thing Sophocles could not have done in the Theban plays was surprise his audience. They were all extremely well acquainted with the plot. There is, of course, a special frisson attendant upon waiting for something to happen that you know is going to happen, and Sophocles, and all traditional authors before him and since, played it for all it is worth. It is worth quite a lot, and it is an experience that is relatively thin in modern novels. But the question worth our attention now is: How did the traditional audience evaluate a telling of a story that they already knew extremely well?

Necessarily, their attention was directed to how the story was told; to the language, to the interpretation, to *what the author had made of it*. When you already know the story, what you appreciate are the essentially literary qualities—language, treatment, the drift of meaning, the symbolic force. By comparison with what was needed to impress the audience with a retelling, satisfying the taste for something original—story-telling for an audience that only wants to know what happens, and wants not to already know—drives the author toward superficiality, silliness, conceits, improbabilities. Satisfying what is fundamentally a decadent taste, the lust for the new, is an impoverishing strategy.

The author's task is inverted; once it was to tell so freshly, so powerfully that the audience would be drawn in, to experience anew, with renewed force, the pity and fear that attended upon the well-known story. Or, of course, even harder to make fresh, the laughter and joy that attended upon the well-known story. But now, handling something novel, a tale never told before, something that the audience knows nothing about until minute by minute you uncover it to them, the problem is the exact opposite. After all, it is trivially obvious that most things that have not happened before are not likely to happen often again; they have a freak quality that robs them of relevance to other lives. The problem is to connect the story to the well-springs of meaning, to give it force and generality, to make it as significant as Cinderella, or Beauty and the Beast, or as resonant as Oedipus cursing wickedness in Thebes, or Moses in the bulrushes, or Figaro discovering his true mother.

To restate. Whereas the art of authorship was once to provide the contingent, the convincing, or charming detail, to flesh out the story, while the story itself provided the deeps of meaning through a symbolic force, the task is now to take the story's newly minted circumstance, detail, and charm, and somehow provide the cosmic depth.

This impossible task is mostly accomplished by cheating. Very few novels are more than superficially novel. The copyright acts do not apply to myths, legends, fairy tales, folk tales, biblical stories, *Beowulf*, which are raided every day, sometimes consciously.

When writing for children one doesn't even have to cover one's tracks. I have done it myself, in *Gaffer Samson's Luck*, for example, in which there is a talisman, a Stone Age arrowhead. I was using an extremely old folk motif in which somebody's life is magically contained in a hidden object, and he is safe as long as the object is safe. I've hedged my bets—you can believe in the magical properties of this object or take it with salt to taste—and I have also inverted the motif; so that the talisman is preserving the Gaffer's life when time has gone by, and it is frustrating his human need to die.

To an astonishing extent you can alter the meaning, the suggested reading, of one of these old tales without losing the traditional symbolism of the tale, very unlike a modern story, which will collapse into something different under the impact of quite small alterations in the structure, a truth that many a film and dramatization has brought home to us. I have twice retold the charming tale of the mermaid of Zennor, a sinister damp lady who kidnapped a chorister for the love of his voice. Once I retold it with dark notes, so as to have him choosing in the end a life beneath the waters, and leaving a pining human on the shore. I told it again recently in *Matthew and the Seasingers,* making it a cheerful story. It works well either way—it isn't a novel.

To return to my assertion that novelists have met the impossible demand upon them by cheating. What I mean by this is that the outlines of the old family drama of folk tale can be discerned repeatedly in great novels. We could have a whole separate exploration of the folk motifs in Shakespeare, by the way, but he is a pre-modern writer, so I shall mention only Perdita, Shakespeare's abandoned child, before turning to novelists for examples. Dickens is full of abandoned children. David Copperfield, for example, is cruelly treated by a wicked stepfather. His mother is too weak to protect him. This isn't even a case of gender inversion, since in the traditional stories it is the same-sex stepparent who persecutes. He runs away to an aunt, a split for his mother, who has all the strength of character the true mother lacks, and is an adequate defender who sees him through to adult life.

Let's turn to Jane Austen, a quintessential rationalist and realist. But what could be clearer than the story line of Cinderella in *Mansfield Park*? Fanny Price is a perfect Cinderella; though her ugly stepsisters are physically beautiful, they are morally ugly. For all her moral beauty, Fanny is not much liked as a heroine for many readers, for she is so limp and abject, sharing Cinderella's disposition to sit in the ashes and make the worst of herself. The story is of course much more complex than a folk tale—there is a false prince as well as a true prince on offer; a profound portrayal of early nineteenth-century, preindustrial English society, its source of wealth, its class system, and much implied comment on women—I won't continue, because this is not a disquisition on Jane Austen, but you get the point.

And isn't there, in Mr. Rochester in *Jane Eyre,* more than a touch of the beast of Beauty and the Beast? As we read the supposedly realist canon of the great novels, don't demon lovers jump up all over the place? Don't dozens of analogous Jacks climb metaphorical beanstalks to fame and fortune? Aren't *Moll Flanders* and *Tom Jones* great hymns to the importance of luck? This is a game anyone can play, and I will leave you all to it.

But the point is that once you start asking authors for originality, then they are desperately strapped for good plots. Re-using the old ones, disguised, is the easiest way out. And I do not mean that this strategy is conscious and deliberate, although it may have been. The author too is steeped in the culture, was brought up on nursery rhyme and folk tale. What seems natural in story-telling is likely to so seem because of the stories one already knows rather than because of a perception of reality.

Was anything then new about the novel? Oh, yes, all sorts of things. Chiefly perhaps the phantasmagoria they offered of real life—a sense of reality profoundly expressive of middle-class circumstances and morality. The folk tale is all about aristocrats and peasants—just imagine one about merchant bankers, millwrights, industrial potters, chartered accountants, and fashion designers. And here, by way of an aside, I should point out to you: So strong is the template for folk tale that a retelling about Beauty and the merchant Banker, or about how Sleeping Beauty refuses the prince, boxes the ears of her wicked stepmother, and marries a footman, can only be a joke. You won't get the joke if you don't know the original story, or one very like it, and that original is only too likely to have more expressive power than the satire. Writing overly feminist versions, for example, is like drawing the bow of Ulysses. (Get the reference? I hope so, because you're on your own for this one.)

The only middle-class person I can remember in a folk tale is Dick Whittington, and he began lowly and rose with the help of a cat. Novels are filled out with ephemeral circumstances. They eschew the shorthand of folk tale in favor of carefully provided background detail. Instead of "there was once a poor woodcutter who had three sons" we have:

> I was born in the year 1632, in the city of York of good family, though not of that country, my father being a foreigner of Bremen who had settled first at Hull. He got a good estate by merchandise, and leaving off his trade, lived afterward at York, from whence he had married my mother, whose relations were named Robinson, a very good family in that country and from whom I was called Robinson Kreutznaer; but by the usual corruption of words in English we are now called, nay, we call ourselves, and write our name Crusoe, and so my companions always called me.
>
> I had two elder brothers, one of which was lieutenant-colonel to an English regiment of foot in Flanders, formally commanded by the famous

Colonel Lockhart, and was killed at the battle
near Dunkirk against the Spaniards; what became
of my second brother I never knew, any more
than my father and mother did know what was
become of me. Being the third son of the family,
and not bred to any trade my head began to be
filled very early with rambling thoughts. . . .

Whatever this famous novel may owe to earlier patterns of
story-telling—to redemption narratives of Christian sin, repen-
tance and salvation—it is spectacularly new in *demeanor*. The
narrative voice has utterly changed. The relationship of story to
actuality, to audience, has gone different. And something about
this difference was so satisfactory that novels became with
breath-taking decisiveness first the dominant popular form, and
then also the dominant elite and prestigious form; thrusting folk
tale into the nursery, and the scholar's study, and poetry into the
purlieus of a very thin upper-crust elite. It seems we all want
prose verisimilitude now.

The other seismic change that overtook story-telling with
the rise of the novel was a change in the choice of protagonists.
You really can have a novel about wicked stepdaughters,
because adult life is now part of the subject. Adults and their
fortunes, miseries, and pleasures figure among protagonists, not
just in relation to some pushy young sprig of a hero or heroine,
but *in themselves*. And surely it was in part the shift of the discourse of stories into adult life that brought about the invention
of a special literature for children.

One of the immense potencies of myth, legend, and folk
tales was that it was always for everybody. And now all tellings
and retellings are felt to be for children; nothing is for everybody. If writers reuse folk motifs in novels—and they do, of
course they do—they disguise it, from readers or perhaps also

from themselves. Where life resembles folk tale, you can be in trouble for imitating life!

You may perhaps lack sympathy for the cultural dilemma of writers, suspended between adult and child, reality and tradition, but the position of writers bears heavily on the next—it is nearly the last—point I would like to make. Who were the tellers of the traditional tales? Those incomparable authors, Trad. and Anon., who were they?

Marina Warner in her recent book *From the Beast to the Blonde* examines gender in the stories, and you might be forgiven for a sense of déjà vu, so many have been the feminist revisitations of the genre. But in fact hers is a profoundly original approach.

Who, and in what social and familial contexts, narrated those tales? Predominantly, though not, of course, exclusively, the narrators—nurses, gossips, grandparents, crones— were women. Old Wives.

"The history of fairy tales, as a form of literature," Warner tells us, "became entangled with changing attitudes to female voices speaking with a claim to knowledge."

Tracking these attitudes, from the high status of sibyls in antiquity, through long centuries of often sadistic rejection of women's voices, we can begin to see the strange ethical world of the fairy tale as the world view of the powerless—the women and children.

That leads to no simple conclusion, because of the strong misogyny of that ethical world: the remorseless stereotyping of the beautiful blonde heroine, the prince-dependent happy endings, the ever absent good mother, and ever present wicked stepmother. "Why," Warner asks, "have women continued to speak at all within this body of story which defames them so profoundly?"

Warner's answer, very broadly, is to restore the narrator,

and the gender of the narrator, to the picture instead of reading the stories out of the family and fireside contexts in which they were told. "Like gossip, fairy tales defame their objects in their attempts to establish—and extend—the speaker's influence."

We can see the cruel stepmothers, the callous half-sisters, the repressive or incestuous fathers (these last edited out by the Brothers Grimm, among others) as projecting women's fears; the fairy coaches, the sudden changes of fortune, the courtship of princes as projecting women's hopes; the magic powers possessed by ugly old crones, by younger children, by orphans of a dead mother, and their sudden acquisition of power as warnings from the weak to the powerful against the abuse of power. The tales are "porous to their tellers' temper and beliefs."

Warner's exposition restores the historical context, the centuries of family life that underlie the stories. She does not so much reject the psychological analysis of Bettelheim and others as she points at its shallow historical sense, its lack of grip on realities other than psychological. Once the historical context of the stories is shorn away, once they lose their connections to the web of tensions in which women were enmeshed, figures like the spoiled princesses, ugly sisters, and so forth grow into archetypes of the human psyche, looking dangerously like the way things are.

Warner's interpretation could transform and focus your reading of fairy tales and *validate* their vision of the world precisely where modern readers may reject it. Do you, for example, loathe the vision of female virtue projected in *Patient Griselda,* or in the silently suffering sister in *The Twelve Brothers*? But, the author reminds us, "Women's capacity for love and action tragically exceeded the permitted boundaries of their lives—this self-immolatory heroism was one of the few chivalrous enterprises open to them." Do you feel scorn for the nonrealistic, fantasy element of the fairy tale? But it is just this that made it possible for them to challenge received views, feel out forbidden ground. It is not because of an animal metamorphosis—a thing that could never happen—that the Donkeyskin tale seems scandalous, but because it adumbrated father-daughter incest, a thing that certainly has happened and will happen again. However anonymous and traditional a story may be, however many thousand times told and retold, it has a context and it has a teller—and the teller is always part of the tale, in spite of all the rumors about the death of the author. In fact, I would like to suggest to you that modern narrative postures, which conceal the author, are also concealing important truths about the stories.

I am going to come to a conclusion by pointing out a curious fact about truth and pattern in narratives. I said above that it was easy to think of Moses in the bulrushes as something that really happened—as plausible and realistic. But the moment one notices that it has a traditional shape—that it very strongly resembles hero stories, abandoned child themes—it becomes, oddly, much harder to accept as a realistic account. People may be very deeply affronted if one points out to them the similarities between John Barleycorn stories and the Osiris story, and the death and resurrection of Christ. As though if a story corresponds to a profound and recurring symbolic truth, it is somehow less likely to be something that really happened. As though a story could be debunked by finding in it a powerful thematic shape.

I believe the boot is on the other foot. Not that a historical story, a story with a modern phantasmagoria of realism, is invalidated as a picture of the external world because it has a traditional symbolic shape, but that these ancient symbolic shapes were formed in the matrix of the real world. The real world does, after all, include ourselves; the inner and the outer dramas of our lives are played out on the same stage. Why should we think that the symbolic truths of the old stories are somehow at odds with the real world? Why should the powerful, recurrent symbolic truth be regarded as evidence against the actuality of something? In the great works of literature both pattern and historicity are present.

Perhaps the most famous, and most troubling, question ever asked was asked by Pilate of Jesus. "What is truth?" he asked.

I don't know the answer. But however different the modern works called novels and the old literature called tales may seem to be, once you resurrect the author and call the author's purposes into view, they may look very similar. I am an old wife now myself, and I am trying to tell the children true stories.

These remarks were made at *Writing the World: Myth as Metaphor,* CLNE at Trinity College, Dublin, Ireland, in 1995.

BREAD, BLOOD, AND WINGS

BARBARA HARRISON

In a published talk given at the Library of Congress, poet and novelist James Dickey described a scene out of his early adolescence. He was walking along a beach in south Georgia with half a loaf of stale bread in his hand. He got to a sandbar where he stopped, tore off a piece of bread, and threw it to a seagull. The gull rose and hovered and came back.

James Dickey stood there tearing small pieces of bread and throwing them into the air when suddenly he was inundated by dozens of seagulls. He was standing on the sandbar covered with wings and beaks, growing more anxious and realizing that he needed to protect himself, but he continued to feed the gulls until his loaf of bread was all gone and the birds were dispersed. In seeking meaning from this incident, and a possible poem, James Dickey says:

> The gulls may—may—be likened to fragments of
> the world which come at the poet from all sides—
> the world's beautiful and dangerous gifts—some-
> times threatening him, not in themselves caring for
> him, but bearing their presences in on him just the

same. The poet is the man with the bread—that is, with the means of attracting them to himself, the bread being the imagination that calls them and feeds them. Again, maybe calling the gulls was my own way of writing on the air: of writing my name on the air with bread, blood, and wings.

Dickey found meaning in the experience, but he did not find a poem. The story serves us in several ways. It provides a metaphor for the nature of the creative process itself, that is the process involved in creating a single poem (or striving to create a poem; he never was able to finish this one), and also a metaphor for the precarious and turbulent childhood and adolescent years that so many books for young readers are about.

The gulls can be taken as fragments of the beautiful, danger-ous, chaotic, and threatening ideas and conceptions that come at the young person from all sides, out of which the youth must cre-ate some sort of meaning. The adolescent is an aspiring poet mold-ing and shaping a vision of the world from thousands of presences, images, and hieroglyphics that inundate and overwhelm him and cry out for some semblance of order, prodding the individual toward reflection and discovery, prompting him to seek some way to write his name on the air with "bread, blood, and wings."

Many artists and writers have talked about the difficulty of the task, the agonizing work, the courage to be one's own tough boss, to be both employer and employee, and the courage to face rejection.

"Risk-taking is the greatest challenge," says Betty Levin. "Being willing to risk words on paper no matter how feeble they might appear. Keep the trash basket nearby," she admonishes.

Above Katherine Paterson's desk a small cache of eleven words—"Before the gates of excellence the high gods have placed sweat"—remind Katherine of what she knows well about the demands of the creative process.

Let's consider for a moment the often exasperating question of children, "Where do you get your ideas?" Why do children ask the question so often? What are children really asking?

They are asking us to explain what might appear to be obvious, but isn't; they are inquiring about inspiration, imagination, talent; they are asking us to explain a mystery.

Perhaps Katherine Paterson's retort to the question "Where do you get your ideas?" is on target. She edges forward in her seat. She leans in the direction of the children crowded around her on the floor. She looks directly into the eyes of the asker and answers, quite simply, "Where do you get *yours*?"

"For the sake of a single verse"—what is required? "For the sake of a single verse," says Rainer Maria Rilke, "one must see many cities, men and things, one must know the animals, one must feel how the birds fly and know the gesture with which the small flowers open in the morning. One must be able to think back to roads in unknown regions, to unexpected meetings and to partings one had long seen coming; to days of childhood that are still unexplained."

"For the sake of a single verse" we investigate the poet's courage to persevere against the tide of misconceptions not only about creativity, about writing in general, and about children's literature, in particular, but also about childhood itself.

By the very act of writing, some children's authors make a political statement. Children cannot be written off. Children are not an undifferentiated mass; they are not nonpersons. They have names and dreams.

We celebrate Robert McCloskey's process of making hundreds of sketches of ducks for *Make Way for Ducklings*, even keeping ducks in his bathtub so that he could study wing structure and temperament.

We contemplate Dr. Seuss's process of writing a thousand pages for every sixty pages of final copy. And his endurance in receiving twenty-nine rejections before the acceptance by Vanguard of his first book, *And to Think That I Saw It on Mulberry Street.*

We stand in awe of J. R. R. Tolkien's flash of illumination when, on the day he was doing the dull and boring work (those are his words) of correcting examination papers, he came across a blank page. He turned the paper over and wrote, "In a hole in the ground there lived a hobbit."

What moves the creator toward the accomplishment of the creation? Is the creation born out of agony? Or longing? Is it born of sustained emotion that suddenly finds expression, or out of compelling determination to be known, to say *Yes, I was here, I lived*?

"Can I turn out to be somebody?" exclaimed Hans Christian Andersen. "I want so badly to be famous."

Is it, as William Faulkner observed, "the artist's way of scribbling 'Kilroy was here' on the wall of the final and irrevocable oblivion through which he must someday pass?"

Is the creative act a way of transcending death? Listen to Emily Dickinson:

> The Only News I know
> Is Bulletins all Day
> From Immortality.
>
> The only Shows I see—
> Tomorrow and Today—
> Perchance Eternity—

Why was Emily Dickinson summoned to the task? Why are some people called while others are not?

And what habits focus the writer's attention on the task at hand? Ernest Hemingway sharpened twenty pencils, Thornton Wilder took long walks, Willa Cather read the Bible because of the inspiration of the language. As an aid to concentration, Gunther Schiller hid rotten apple parings in his desk. Walter de la Mare smoked and W. H. Auden drank endless cups of tea. It's not an interest in the number of pencils that Hemingway sharpened or cups of tea that Auden drank that becomes noteworthy; it's the enormous demands of concentration.

In his article, "The Making of a Poem," Stephen Spender contrasts the processes of concentration of Mozart and Beethoven. Mozart figured things out in his head often while walking in his garden or on trips, and then he put his thoughts on paper—a whole complete work would tumble onto the page. Beethoven, on the other hand, kept notebooks in which he wrote fragments of themes, often working and reworking them over years. Scholars have been startled by the clumsiness of Beethoven's first ideas.

Spender points out that what counts in both cases is the capacity of the artist to pursue and to attain his vision.

Vision, concentration, and memory are the patterns that Dickey, Spender, and Rilke refer to. But also ask Penelope Lively about vision. Ask Virginia Hamilton about concentration. Ask Susan Cooper about memory; she is still haunted by childhood memories of war.

"For the sake of a single verse . . . one must be able to think back to days of childhood that are still unexplained. . . . For it is not yet the memories themselves. Not till they have turned to blood within us, to glance and gesture, nameless and no longer to be distinguished from ourselves—not till then can it happen that in a most rare hour the first word of a verse arises in their midst and goes forth from them."

These remarks were made at *Image and Word: Patterns of Creativity*, CLNE at Mount Holyoke College, South Hadley, Massachusetts, in 1994.

SEEING THE LION

MARGARET MAHY

Early on the morning on which I began thinking, most intently, about the opening of this talk, I became aware that my four cats were clustering and staring at me in a significant way, and cat owners among you will realize that this scrutiny—this atmosphere of silent expectation edging into reproach—can become increasingly intrusive. There is probably some primitive telepathic element involved. I stumped irritably to the refrigerator in search of cat food, and realized as I looked at the kitchen bench in the inching, sullen light of a winter's morning that within about twenty minutes Gloria, my neighbor and occasional housekeeper, would be calling in to tidy up after me, and that, as ever, I must conceal from her what a pig I really am . . . though I think she has a pretty good and tactfully suppressed idea by now.

I quickly wiped some mud from the top of the microwave oven, bundled dishes into the dishwasher while hastily eating (since wasting food was a primary crime in my childhood) the scraps left over from the night before . . . the sort of debris that gets pushed into the back of the fridge so that you can make soup out of it on the weekend, and that mutates into an alien life form within a mere couple of months. I ate a piece of apple, turning slightly brown, a sausage, the remains of last night's salad, and, although it was half past eight in the morning I drank what was left in a wine bottle (not much, I hasten to add) without once pausing to think about its bouquet, possibly just as well since the British weekly magazine *New Scientist* spoke in a 1995 article (an article giving scientific reasons for the excellence of New Zealand white wine) of New Zealand's astonishingly successful "Sauvignon Blanc characterized by the herbaceous flavor of gooseberries, and capsicum and the aroma of cut grass and tom cat spray." (It then went on to say that the aroma has been attributed to nitrogen-containing methoxpyrazenes. It made me glad I am not a sensitive connoisseur.)

Anyhow, on this occasion I merely swallowed the last of the wine, and virtuously tidied the empty bottle into the recycling box on top of the washing machine. As I did this I was frowning and puzzling over what I could possibly say in my talk today. Endings and beginnings was suggesting something in itself, but I was not quite sure what. Ten minutes later I was suddenly filled with a strange elation—probably due to the sausage—and began to sing Tom Lehrer's song "Fight Fiercely Harvard," which I know by heart. Early in August I would actually be at Harvard—that mythological place—and I would be in mythological company too. The theme of the conference— Endings and Beginnings—had a welcome resonance, and part of the fascination of trying to work out a talk like this is the moment of sudden enlightenment when you know the clockwork of your ideas has inched forward another cog or two.

Anyhow, under the influence of that sausage, I began to think, as I carried other scraps (things that even my parents wouldn't have expected me to eat) out to the compost heap, that endings were often implicit in beginnings, and that part of the writer's job, on getting an idea, was to detect the compressed ending, to tease it out, to coax it into public view . . . or perhaps to goad the beginning out of the end, for sometimes one gets the idea for the ending first. "String theories," says Stephen Hawking, "are only consistent if space-time has ten or twenty-six dimensions, but it may be that we only notice the three space dimensions and a single time one because the others are curled up in a very, very small space . . . something like a million, million, million, millionth of an inch." (I quote directly here.) Perhaps endings are compressed into beginnings in rather the same way. Of course we think of writers beginning at the beginning, going on to the end and then stopping, but it isn't always like that. In her Newbery acceptance speech, let me remind you, Susan Cooper described the evolution of *The Dark Is Rising* sequence, and the way in which she came to see that the story she had to tell would work its way out through five narratives. "One was already written. Four more were to come," she says in her speech, "so I made an outline of each, characters and plot and setting, and before I started to write the second, *The Dark Is Rising,* I wrote the very last page of the very last book. That is still sitting in my file and I shall use it unchanged—when I find myself reluctantly reaching the place where it belongs later this year."

You don't make this sort of connection at twenty to nine in the morning if you have restricted your breakfast to cornflakes.

As I tossed pumpkin skin and soup bones into the compost heap, I thought about the beginning of a story that was, in a way, my own beginning—my own beginning as a published writer, that is—that first story of mine that I ever saw magically change into a book, a transmutation that I had imagined so often that, when it came about, it seemed like the inevitable fulfillment of a prophesy, and yet a fulfillment so frail, so contingent, I could hardly believe it had ever been achieved. This book, one of the shortest stories I have ever written, was called

The Lion in the Meadow, and was first published in 1969—published in the U.S.A. too, for New Zealand publishers in those days could rarely afford to produce picture books in a country where bookshops were so dominated by British books. Indeed, the small market, and the limited expectations they had, made it mandatory that any book published within the country should have a strong New Zealand background. For a variety of reasons, partly because my own childhood reading was so predominantly British, my own first stories were set in nowhere—or rather in some dimension in which all stories, regardless of settings, flowed comfortably together. At some level, not a conscious one, I did not think my own country or my own life were appropriate subjects for stories, and any attempts on my part to establish a local habitation for imaginary people and events became unconvincing and somehow boring to me. After all, I was, as all authors are, not only the writer of the story but the first reader—the first listener too.

Back in 1964 I began writing a story that I thought was going to be a really good one. I wrote it in pieces over about a week, and as it happened (as it was *meant* to happen, Kurt Vonnegut would suggest) I finished this story early in the evening. Writing, when the writer feels the work is going well, when the words are flowing and the story is a strong one, can be a god-like experience. One has to realize, even as one is experiencing it, that this is a delusory feeling, and is used to justify a lot of bad art. Nevertheless Tolkien, in his essay in *Tree and Leaf,* suggests that it is quite appropriate—that creatively writing men and women are fulfilling at a secondary level their true nature as beings created in the image of God, himself a notable creator. Anyhow there I was, early in the evening, my story finished as far as I wanted to take it just then, yet still charged with energy of invention, and wanting to go on writing. Anything and everything seemed possible. Suddenly I was magical—I could go in any direction. All the journey needed was a first step. Snatching up my pen once more, I wrote a first line: "The little boy said to his mother, 'Mother, there is a lion in the meadow.'"

Well—I had my beginning.

I had no idea where these words might lead me. I wrote the next line and then the next, improvising in what turned out to be a particularly useful way. The final story is still one of the most economical texts I have ever produced, and I am still particularly pleased with it for that reason, since I know myself to be a wordy writer, and it is not a characteristic I admire. "The story wrote itself," I have heard writers saying, but stories don't write themselves. Writers say this when they want to suggest they have been singled out for divine possession, and also because it is an accurate way of describing a certain sort of writing experience. The best accounts acknowledge the visionary nature of experience, but joke about it. (Jokes can be noble, I think.) In Russell Hoban's book *Kleinzeit*, Kleinzeit, an incipient writer, opens the door of the yellow paper's cage and it springs out at him.

> Over and over they rolled together, bloody and roaring. Doesn't matter what the title is to start with, he said, anything will do. HERO I'll call it. Chapter one. He wrote the first page while the yellow paper clawed his guts. The pain was blinding. It'll kill me, said Kleinzeit, there's no surviving this. He wrote the second line, the third, completed the first paragraph. The roaring and the blood stopped, the yellow paper rubbed purringly against his leg, the first paragraph danced and sang, leaped and played on the green grass in the dawn. Up the Athenians, said Kleinzeit, and went to sleep.

In my case, I wrote to the end of my second story—the unexpected one. Up the Athenians, I said, or words to that effect, and went to sleep.

Two weeks later, rereading the two stories, I found, rather to my surprise, that the second, shorter story was the one I liked best. The longer story has never been published, yet in a way I still feel the energies that went into the writing of it now compacted in *A Lion in the Meadow*. A pole vaulter runs before he or she vaults. Then he or she soars up towards the bar, hoisted high on the bending pole which he or she then releases, and the force of the preceding run is transformed into upward flight, weightlessness, and the enchanted efficiency of the final run over the bar. The transference of energy from the run, to the leap on the bending pole, to the final flight and twist, make a useful analogy for the process that marked the beginning of *A Lion in the Meadow*. I don't think I have ever written a story so instinctively . . . so easily. It was not the end of the surprises this simple story had to offer me.

Sometime after I had become used to the idea that I was actually the author of a book, I was suddenly seized with a great curiosity to know what it would be like to read this story for the first time. It is a curiosity impossible for the writer to satisfy. The story he or she has written has probably been revised and written out again and again, and can never return to the state of being totally unknown. Nevertheless I decided to trick myself, as far as was possible, into reading my own story as if I were a casual reader, picking the book off a library shelf, making an accidental contact, and accepting or rejecting it accordingly. After all, this is the moment to which the story has been directed . . . the moment when it springs out of a book and becomes the reader's story.

I knew just where *A Lion in the Meadow* was on my bookshelf. I walked past the bookshelf, not looking at the books on it, and then, pretending I was really interested in something else, trailed my fingers over the backs of the books until I found the one I knew so well. I pulled it off the shelf and carried it into my bedroom, whistling and glancing left and right, still pretending to think of other things, and deliberately refusing to glance down at the cover in case I was jolted into a state of familiarity too soon. The moment of truth came. Opening the book at random, I looked down, quickly and ruthlessly, and read the first words I saw. "The little boy said to his mother, 'Mother, there is a big, roaring, yellow, whiskery lion in the meadow.'"

Then, overwhelmingly, I remembered something I had not thought about for many years . . . certainly not at the time when I was writing the story. I remembered myself as a small child, three years old, sitting on my father's knee and listening to a series of stories he invented evening after evening, all unrecallable now, except for the opening line, which was always the same. "Once upon a time there was a great big black-maned Abyssinian lion." I stood transfixed, staring down at the page.

I remember that beginning, only the beginning, repeated night after night, and it suddenly seemed to me that the lion in my story was the same lion my father had given me all those years ago, and my own story, the one I had written, had been packed into a million, million, million, million, millionth of an inch inside its own opening line. I had not been inventing at all. I had been pushed by the energy of the moment into a secret remembering and reconstruction. The big, roaring, yellow, whiskery lion and the great big, black-maned Abyssinian lion certainly moved to the same beat. So, by now, it seems that the first story I remember hearing was in some way the story of the first book I had ever published. In contemplating an ending, the achievement of an ambition I had entertained since I was seven, I had been returned to a beginning.

Of course for me at least this is a satisfying story within itself. There is a fictional balance and fulfillment in it. But in order to get command of many true parts of our lives and make them communicable we do turn them into stories. This "storying" can enable us to work out, to some extent at least, what is going on. My granddaughter has certainly cast herself as heroine. "Do you mind looking after us?" she once began to ask me, but rapidly edited her question out, replacing it with an assertion. "How lovely for you to have the chance of looking after us," she said instead. We all edit our stories, stretch them, shape them, and emphasize useful correspondences. We choose certain significant events, forgetting others, as we build up our private system of clues and passwords, work our way through many calculations to final, fertile equations. Energy ultimately equals not m but ms, manuscript, multiplied by the speed of light squared. We listen to stories with pleasure because, as we work our way from beginning to ending, we are telling ourselves, moment by moment, our own tales, and we all need the models . . . we all need the practice.

A story is seldom published to universal applause. Over the years *A Lion in the Meadow* has been criticized for various imperfections . . . for using the word "meadow" (which is not part of average New Zealand terminology; a New Zealander would almost certainly say "paddock") and as being sexist because the mother is the one who is at home peeling the potatoes. But the criticism I have had most occasion to think about concerns the ending of *A Lion in the Meadow*, which I have thought about every bit as much as I have ever thought about its beginning, though for different, more external reasons.

As it was originally written, it ends in a ruthless way. The mother, who did not take stories seriously, had patronizingly invented a story about a dragon in a matchbox—a story in which she certainly did not believe—to trick her child into less distracting behavior. Almost at once she was rebuked. Stories suddenly roared into life around her. The lion, in which she had not believed, suddenly becomes actual, rushes into the kitchen crying, "Hide me! A dragon is after me," and hides in the broom cupboard. The mother, horrified at the turn events have taken, protests, "But there wasn't a real dragon. It was just a story I made up." "It turned out to be true after all," her child explains to her. "You should have looked in the matchbox first." The child and the lion then go off together, and the tale ends by saying, "The mother never made up a story again." Or, once upon a time, the story ended like that. Once upon a time the mother learned that stories have power beyond parental condescension.

"Do you think the mother really saw the lion?" my first editor asked me curiously. I replied that I did. "But that doesn't make sense," she said. "A lion doesn't suddenly materialize out of nothing. The artist will draw the pictures so that the reader can make up his or her own mind." I was perfectly happy about that. At that stage in my writing life if she had suggested that the lion be replaced by a pink elephant I might have agreed with her in the most servile fashion. I was so keen to be published I didn't have as much integrity back then as I can afford now. But I genuinely *liked* the ambiguity of the idea, and, since I don't want to be a submissive reader, I can't afford to be a dictatorial writer, either. And yet I was puzzled. After all the editor was right, and, even in these days of e-mail and the Internet and three-dimensional imaging, lions don't materialize out of nothing. Anyone who praises rationality as often as I do has to acknowledge that. All the same, at some level I felt certain the mother had seen the lion, and *had* been overwhelmed by it. *Seeing the lion* . . . it sounds like some poetic Chinese phrase used to designate something prosaic. (I was recently told that Chinese commentators said of an apartment block, which tragically collapsed in Kuala Lumpur because an underground stream was running through its foundations, that it had been built on the back of the dragon.) *Seeing the lion!* The mother never made up a story again, because she had *seen the lion*, and she kept on seeing it.

But who would understand any of that, especially in a simple children's story? You have to work your way toward such possibilities which, we all know, are compacted into a million million million millionth of an inch, and I would not have rationalized it in this way if it had not been for a particular result in the outside world—the criticism of the final line, the effect this criticism had on me and, in due course, on the book.

As the story began its public life, I was sometimes reproached, usually quite gently, for telling a story with such a negative conclusion, and the people who expressed dismay were people whose opinions I respected—fellow librarians and editors, people on whose judgment the continuance of the story depended. "I love the story," a librarian acquaintance once said to me, "but I can't bear to read the ending." I began to feel rather guilty because of these judgments. Some sixteen years after the story had first been published, the publisher proposed a new edition with new illustrations by the original artist, and I was asked to come up with a kinder, more positive ending. I agreed to this with a certain relief, feeling I was being given a chance to correct something that I had not got right the first time. In due course the new edition appeared, and immediately, along with those who expressed pleasure at the altered ending, I began to hear from people who were indignant at the change, who felt, in some way, betrayed because they had trusted the story the way it had been told the *first* time. I think they were right to feel like this, for I also found that, though I had so willingly altered the ending, I did not believe my own alteration. Now I consider *A Lion in the Meadow* very cautiously, feeling the ruthlessness of the first ending still lurking under the second, kinder one, and believing it to be the true ending. Don't patronize the story, the outer sign of the pattern you are destined to fulfill . . . don't use it in the wrong way or it will have its revenge. It might pull itself out of your life and you will never make up a story again. Or it might rush into your kitchen and take over the broom cupboard. Every time you go to that cupboard, planning to sweep the floor, it will look out and roar at you. You will never make up a story again, because now you know you are living eye-to-eye with story every moment of your everyday life.

Once again it is only a subsequent puzzling, brought on by the questions of others and response to my own reactions, that has made me conjecture in this way. I suppose that many writers write, as I do, out of an unreasonable expectation . . . that a reader will live with the story on and off over many years and that the story will change, grow, and stretch with them, and that, as the reader changes, the story will change too—not in its words but in the span of its meaning.

I don't see anything wrong in writing with this hope, though one certainly should not depend on it. I am the sort of reader who reads like this, and I know I am not alone in returning to stories and suddenly discovering something new in them, perhaps because I have brought something new to them as reader, or because the author has hidden something there that I have only just recognized. I don't think I am a particularly unusual reader in this way. I am one of a multitude; these days I read to my grandchildren stories that I had read to me in my own childhood. I am entering an *ending* stage of reading aloud (because I don't like my chances of ever surviving to read to great-grandchildren, particularly if I keep tidying up so efficiently at half past eight in the morning). Anyhow, I remember having some of these same stories read to me when I was little, and also remember reading them to my own children. A history of contact makes the story I am reading one thing to me and another to the small listeners. *I* feel, as they cannot, the force of all those previous encounters building up in the simple words, and I feel such a charge of emotion that I weep over slight stories, jokey and happy ones, while my grand-children stare at me curiously, for tears to them are associated with sadness, not with an accumulated power, the roar of an inner lion, so potent and forcible that one's nervous system cannot cope. These are beginnings for the little children, and the stories work for them just as their authors intended. The children laugh or are intrigued. "Say it again!" they order me. But the stories are alive, secretly growing and expanding, branching out, forming and reforming. Here they are being told, yet again, in ways peculiar to me, an individual reader who has lived with these tales and is ending with them.

Endings and beginnings . . . our own beginnings and our own endings are stories all tangled with the beginnings and endings of other stories. It is the writer's job to find an ending, perhaps to decide just which ending from several possible end-ings is the correct one to present in print—to externalize—for, after the choice is made, the ending seems inevitable and *true*, categorical rather than contingent.

At any rate, if my own beginnings have affected the begin-nings of my stories, it is also true that stories seriously affected my beginnings. On other occasions I have described the alarm-ing incursions that story made into my childhood when I was less able to defend myself from fictional suggestion. I have talked about—not the book, but the film of—*The Jungle Book* (the version starring Sabu), which crashed into my undefended life, utterly amazing me and causing me to assert publicly that I could talk the language of the animals, something that every other child in the school knew to be untrue. Not only that, I knew it too, but I set out to prove my oneness with animal cre-ation. Challenged, I talked gibberish to passing dogs who glanced at me contemptuously and went their own ways. I tried to show my animal sympathy by drinking out of puddles and eating leaves. Children would come up to me in the playground at school, bringing leaves of various kinds, and saying "Eat this!" and I ate them all without hesitation. I don't know how long this went on . . . not very long because I was also embarrassed at what I found myself doing and, increasingly, knew it to be a poor, scruffy construction compared with the magnificent truth of the story. I may have behaved like this anywhere between six weeks or three months, and yet now, when I think of my elementary-school years, I find they are utterly dominated by this memory. Much of the rest has been edited out, and at some unconscious level I have picked on this as the central image of my early school life. It is not as if I enjoyed the experience, and for many years was so ashamed of it—the assumption of a role that convinced no one, and even bewildered me to some extent—that I refused to think about it. I certainly never discussed it in any way. Why did I cling so persistently to this invented fable? I knew I could not speak the language of animals, but in some way, having contacted the story of Mowgli and incorporated it in the silent inner realm, it seemed too wonderful to be left there. I wanted to drag it from its proper place into the world of talking, and force it to be real there, too. I saw the lion, one might say, which should have been enough for me, but I wanted everyone else to see it too, and to agree that I was in charge of it.

Officially *The Other Side of Silence* began when I read an account by Russ Rhymer in *The New Yorker* of the life of the closet child Genie, her language deprivation due to extended childhood abuse, the academic competition to study her deprivation and possible emergence from it, and the final neglect that followed her exploitation. It is a fascinating story in itself, and because of the impact *The Jungle Book* made on me, I have over the years followed the debate about language acquisition with a general interest, read accounts of all kinds of true and semi-true people like the wolf children, Amala and Kamala, the wild boy of Aveyron, and others. In my case, once given the push by the article by Russ Rhymer, I found, as writers often do I imagine, a lot of stories rushing in eager to feed into the emerging tale . . . gothic horror stories, anecdotes of the strange house in the wood, and of the member of the family mad and desolate in the locked room upstairs. There were parallels in Genie's story and that of *Jane Eyre.*

Mixed in with these were my own beginnings—the childhood memories of picking my way from one tree to another along the lines of wattles and pines that defined the boundaries of my father's timber yard, talking to imaginary animals, but of course really talking to myself, babbling and inventing a language of sounds and signs while checking up on bird's nests, certain the birds would realize my interest in them was kindly, quite sure they were too rational to be placed under any stress because of my visits. I seemed to have acknowledged, at last, that puddle-drinking child I had been ashamed of for so many years, but I changed her into the cloudy, mysterious heroine who had also been with me for a long time. There they are, both of them, in *The Other Side of Silence*, and along with the heroine's Mowgli-ish preoccupation goes an adult acknowledgment of what a wolf child like Mowgli, a human brought up without human language, might really have been like.

As I was writing this tale, I began to be aware of something disconcerting. I was embarking on a story whose time had come. Suddenly there were various stories of various silences appearing in the world ahead of mine. *Blabbermouth*, a funny story by the Australian writer Maurice Gleitzman, was the first of which I was aware. There are curious parallels with the Jodie Foster film *Nell*, which I have only heard discussed. After my own story was written, I read *Knowledge of Angels*. The underlying story—

the deep story—was never mine in the first place, but existed like some platonic form, generating a variety of individual stories, all presented in widely differing ways. But my story seemed different enough, I think—partly drama, partly joke, partly game with words, and partly a remembrance of things past . . . not too separated from *A Lion in the Meadow* really. This ending certainly has connections with the long-ago beginning.

As adults and writers, while we work toward the ending coded into us, it may be that our beginnings curl up and hide themselves in us. They are still there and still real, but perhaps compressed into a million million million million millionth of an inch.

I originally planned to finish this talk by telling a story—a story in rhyme that I know by heart. There is a pleasure in being released from the tyranny of print and the page . . . to feel the words coming, it seems, out of nowhere . . . to give the illusion of instantaneous invention with something that has taken a lot of hidden work and calculation. For even though one knows that one has worked and worked to produce structure and order, when the finished story is contained in memory it seems to have re-entered the place it originally came from—an invisible realm— a collective human imagination in which proto-stories live, waiting for connections to be made, waiting to take form according to the judgment and history of the individual who has made the connection. However, I found I could not follow my original plan because, as I came to think about *The Other Side of Silence*, I began to see seductive connections with *A Lion in the Meadow* . . . between ending and beginning. Are these connections really there? Well, I certainly believe in them now I have made them.

Toward the end of the book, the heroine of *The Other Side of Silence* (a girl called Hero, incidentally) adds a postscript to the mixture of biography, family story, and gothic drama she has been slowly putting together (drawing a distinction between real events and true ones as she does). The ending is too long to quote in full, but I have connected some pieces together, along with a description of her actions on completing her postscript. This is what she says:

> If things were fair, all stories would be anonymous. I don't mean that the story-teller wouldn't get paid for telling. But there would be no names on the covers of books or interviews on television . . . just the story itself, climbing walls, sliding from tree to tree and stealing secretly through the forest of the world, real but more than real. Set free from the faults that go with the author's name. Made true. But of course things aren't fair. They never have been.
>
> Once I used to pick up *Old Fairy Tales*, shut my eyes, put my blind finger blindly on a line, then open my eyes suddenly so that I could read whatever it was Fate had to say to me. TELL YOUR SORROWS TO THE OLD STOVE IN THE CORNER I read, because true life is timeless and the story already knew what lay ahead of me. And when the story gives you good advice there's no way out. You just have to act upon it.

And indeed the heroine, called Hero, does tell her sorrows to the old stove in the corner. This is what she does:

> Hero looked at what she had set down on the screen, but she did not print it out. Instead she picked up her thick manuscript, weighed it in her hands, then moved over to the wood stove on its square of deep-blue tiles. She opened the black door with the glass panel set in it, and pushed the block of pages in, turning her head

away, perhaps making sure she would not be tempted to snatch them out again. Thick smoke suddenly gushed out towards her, not rising into the air at once, but pouring downward. The pages were too thick to burn easily, but, as she prodded them with a poker, coughing and fanning the smoke away from her face with her left hand, they began to smolder at the edges. She separated them from one another as well as she could. A few caught fire; others followed. By the time she closed the door of the wood burner her story was roaring like a lion in the long throat of the stove pipe.

So Hero stood there listening to her private lion and the family voices coming up the stairs from below. She imagined her story leaping into the sky, shaking its mane of smoke, and then slowly dissolving over the city and becoming not just one but many stories.

Copying these pieces down I found myself thinking that before she set that lion free to roar, not in the broom cupboard but the stove pipe—before she told her stories to the old stove in the corner as the fairy tale instructed her to do—Hero had actually seen the lion. Now she and the story were, at some level, one and the same thing. Through writing and reading she had reached a point where she would never need to make up a story again, because she was now at one with the platonic form with which we continually dance, inventing one another as we whirl. Have I invented stories or have stories invented me? Is this true or another bit of academic trickery . . . a meaning dragged out of nothing? The truth is I don't know. It is true I once pulled a copy of my own first book off the shelf, opened it at random, read a line, and took serious notice of the story connection I then made, just as the heroine of *The Other Side of*

Silence does. It is also true that I have burned books—though usually because I knew they were so faulty they needed to be put out of the agony that existence in paper and print had imposed on them, and returned to that earlier state. It is true that, as a child, I drank from puddles and ate leaves with a sort of confused intensity, trying to make myself one with a story. And it is true that the lion is there—the lion of the story I suppose—the great big black-maned Abyssinian lion—still roaring and shaking its mane. Genuinely it seemed that, as I thought about this talk, ending and beginning had rushed together, and crowded out the original intention. *Why shouldn't I go ahead and tell this other story anyway. Why would it matter? This isn't a lecture—it's an after-dinner talk—it's for fun.* But this talk had turned out to be like a story in itself—it has "moved meaningfully step by step with cause and effect through time to a consummation, an ending that makes sense in light of all that comes before."

Perhaps the theme of endings and beginnings, initially intensified by eating early-morning sausage, was sufficient to make a story out of this talk. I don't think there is anything remarkable in these connections. . . . I think that any writer, any reader, can give themselves a structure through stories, using, often unconsciously using, selection and emphasis. And in some important ways

> What we call the beginning is often the end
> And to make an end is to make a beginning.
> The end is where we start from.

These remarks were made at *Endings and Beginnings: The Shape of Story,* CLNE at Harvard University, Cambridge, Massachusetts, in 1996.

EARTHSEA REVISIONED

URSULA K. LE GUIN

In our hero-tales of the Western world, heroism has been gendered: The hero is a man.

Women may be good and brave, but with rare exceptions (Spenser, Ariosto, Bunyan?) women are not heroes. They are sidekicks. Never the Lone Ranger, always Tonto. Women are seen in relation to heroes: as mother, wife, seducer, beloved, victim, or rescuable maiden. Women won independence and equality in the novel, but not in the hero-tale. From the *Iliad* to the *Song of Roland* to *The Lord of the Rings*, right up into our lifetime, the hero-tale and its modern form, heroic fantasy, have been a male preserve: a sort of great game-park where Beowulf feasts with Teddy Roosevelt, and Robin Hood goes hunting with Mowgli, and the cowboy rides off into the sunset alone. Truly a world apart.

Since it's about men, the hero-tale has concerned the establishment or validation of manhood. It has been the story of a quest, or a conquest, or a test, or a contest. It has involved conflict and sacrifice. Archetypal configurations of the hero-tale are the hero himself, of course, and often the night sea journey, the wicked witch, the wounded king, the devouring mother, the wise old man, and so on. (These are Jungian archetypes; without devaluing Jung's immensely useful concept of the archetype as an essential mode of thought, we might be aware that the archetypes he identifies are mindforms of the Western European psyche as perceived by a man.)

When I began writing heroic fantasy, I knew what to write about. My father had told us stories from Homer before I could read, and all my life I'd read and loved the hero-tales. That was my own tradition, those were my archetypes, that's where I was at home. Or so I thought until—in the enchanting phrase of my youth—sex reared its ugly head.

The late sixties ended a long period during which artists were supposed to dismiss gender, to ignore it, to be ignorant of what sex they were. For many decades it had been held that to perceive oneself as a woman writer or as a man writer would limit one's scope, one's humanity; that to write as a woman or as a man would politicize the work and so invalidate its universality. Art was to transcend gender. This idea of genderlessness or androgyny is what Virginia Woolf said was the condition of the greatest artists' minds. To me it is a demanding, a valid, a permanent ideal.

But over against the ideal, the fact was that the men in charge of criticism, the colleges, and the society had produced male definitions of both art and gender. And these definitions were set above question. The standards themselves were gendered. Men's writing was seen as transcending gender, women's writing as trapped in it. Why am I using the past tense?

And so the only way to have one's writing perceived as above politics, as universally human, was to gender one's writing male. Writing as a man, to male standards of what is universally human, was centralized, privileged; writing as a woman was marginalized. Masculine judgment of art was definitive; feminine perception and option was secondary, second-rate. Therefore, Virginia Woolf also warned us that a woman's writing will not be adequately judged so long as the standards of judgment are established and defended by men. And this is in the present tense, as it was sixty years ago.

Well, then, if art, if language itself doesn't belong to women, women can only borrow it or steal it. *Le vol:* flighty, women are. Thieves, fly-by-nights. Off on their broomsticks.

And why should men listen to stolen stories unless they concern important things—that is, the doings of men? Children, of course, even manchildren, are supposed to listen to women. Part of women's work is telling stories to children. Unimportant work, but important stories. Stories of the heroes.

From the general to the personal: Since my Earthsea books were published as children's books, I was in an approved female role. So long as I behaved myself, obeyed the rule, I was free to enter the heroic realm. I loved that freedom and never gave a thought to the terms of it. Now that I know that even in Fairyland there is no escape from politics, I look back and see that I was writing partly by the rules, as an artificial man, and partly against the rules, as an inadvertent revolutionary. Let me add that this isn't a confession or a plea for forgiveness. I like my books. Within the limits of my freedom I was free; I wrote well; and subversion need not be self-aware to be effective.

To some extent I pushed against the limits. For example, I followed the intense conservatism of traditional fantasy in giving Earthsea a rigid social hierarchy of kings, lords, merchants, peasants; but I colored all the good guys brown or black. Only the villains were white. I saw myself as luring white readers to identify with the hero, to get inside his skin and only then find it was a dark skin. I meant this as a strike against racial bigotry. I think now that my subversion went further than I knew, for by making my hero dark-skinned I was setting him outside the whole European heroic tradition, in which heroes are not only male but white. I was making him an Outsider, an Other, like a woman, like me.

(You will not see that dark man on most of the covers of the Earthsea books, by the way; publishers insist that jackets showing black people "kill sales," and forbid their artists to color the hero darker than tan. Look at the jackets of Alice Walker's or Paule Marshall's novels to realize how strong this taboo is. I think it has affected many readers' perception of Ged.)

I had a vanilla villainess in the first book, but in the sequel it was my heroine who was white. I'm not sure why. I'd made the Kargish people white in the first book, and had to stick to it; but perhaps also I simply lacked the courage to make my heroine doubly Other.

In *The Tombs of Atuan*, Arha/Tenar is not a hero, she is a heroine. The two English words are enormously different in their implications and value; they are indeed a wonderful exhibition of how gender expectations are reflected (created) by linguistic usage.

Tenar, a heroine, is not a free agent. She is trapped in her situation. And when the hero comes, she becomes complementary to him. She cannot get free of the Tombs without him.

But—a fact some critics ignore—neither can Ged get free without her. They are interdependent. I redefined my hero by making him dependent, not autonomous. But heroines are always dependent, not autonomous—even a Fidelio. They act only with and for their man. I had reimagined the man's role, but not the woman's. I had not yet thought what a female hero might be.

No wonder; where are the women in Earthsea? Two of the books of the trilogy have no major female characters, and in all three the protagonists, in the precise sense of the word, are male. Communities of men in Earthsea are defined as powerful, active, and autonomous; the community of women in Atuan is described as obedient to distant male rulers, a static, closed society. No change can come, nothing can be done, until a man arrives. Hero and heroine depend on each other in getting free of this terrible place, but the man originates the action of the book.

And in all three books the fundamental power, magic, belongs to men; only to men; only to men who have no sexual contact with women.

The women of Earthsea have skills and powers and may be in touch with obscure earth-forces, but they aren't wizards or mages. They know, at most, a few words of the language of power, the Old Speech; they are never methodically taught it by the men who do know it. There are no women at the School of Wizardry at Roke. At best, women are village witches. But that's at worst, too, for the saying is quoted more than once: "Weak as women's magic, wicked as women's magic."

So, no women in college, no women in power, and that's how things are in Marlboro country. Nobody said anything about it, when the books first came out.

The tradition I was writing in was a great one, a strong one. The beauty of your own tradition is that it carries you. It flies, and you ride it. Indeed, it's hard not to let it carry you, for it's older and bigger and wiser than you are. It frames your thinking and puts winged words in your mouth. If you refuse to ride, you have to stumble along on your own two feet; if you try to speak your own wisdom, you lose that wonderful fluency. You feel like a foreigner in your own country, amazed and troubled by things you see, not sure of the way, not able to speak with authority.

It is difficult for a woman to speak or write with authority unless she remains within a traditional role, since authority is still granted and withheld by the institutions and traditions of men (such as this amazing medieval institution where we are guests this week, on whose august lawns Virginia Woolf was forbidden to walk). A woman, as queen or prime minister, may for a time fill a man's role; that changes nothing. Authority is male. It is a fact. My fantasy dutifully reported the fact.

But is that all a fantasy does—report facts?

Readers and reviewers of the trilogy did not question Ged's masculinity, as far as I know. He was seen as thoroughly manly. And yet he had no sex life at all. This is of course traditional in the hero-tale: the hero may get a pro-forma bride as final reward, but from Samson and Delilah to Merlin and Nimue to the war stories of our century, sexuality in the hero is shown not as prowess but as weakness. Strength lies in abstinence—the avoidance of women and the replacement of sexuality by non-sexual male bonding.

The establishment of manhood in heroic terms involves the absolute devaluation of women. The women's touch, in any sense, threatens that heroic masculinity.

By the early seventies, when I finished the third book of Earthsea, traditional definitions and values of masculinity and femininity were all in question. I'd been questioning them myself in other books. Women readers were asking how come all the wise guys on the Isle of the Wise were guys. The artist who was above gender had been exposed as a man hiding in a raincoat. No serious writer could, or can, go on pretending to be genderless. I couldn't continue my hero-tale until I had, as woman and artist, wrestled with the angels of the feminist consciousness. It took me a long time to get their blessing. From 1972 on I knew there should be a fourth book of Earthsea, but it was sixteen years before I could write it.

The fourth book, *Tehanu*, takes up where the trilogy left off, in the same hierarchic, male-dominated society; but now, instead of using the pseudo-genderless male viewpoint of the heroic tradition, the world is seen through a woman's eyes. This time the gendering of the point of view is neither hidden nor denied. In Adrienne Rich's invaluable word, I had "revisioned" Earthsea.

Earlier in this conference, Jill Paton Walsh suggested that in *Tehanu* I was "doing penance." Irredeemably secular, I'd call it affirmative action. In my lifetime as a writer, I have lived through a revolution, a great and ongoing revolution. When the world turns over, you can't go on thinking upside down. What was innocence is now irresponsibility. Visions must be revisioned.

In Atuan, Tenar lived in a world apart, a tiny desert community of women and eunuchs; she knew nothing beyond it. This setting was in part a metaphor of the "innocence" long instituted as the value of a girl, her "virtue" (the word deriving from *vir*, man, her worth to men being her only worth). That book and that innocence ended as she entered the "great world" of men and their doings. In *Tehanu*, she has lived in that world for years and knows her part of it well, the part she chose. She chose to leave the mage Ogion, her guardian and guide to masculine knowledge; she chose to be a farmer's wife. Why? Was she seeking a different, an obscurer knowledge? Was she being "womanly," bowing to society's resistance to independently powerful women?

Tenar certainly considers herself independent and responsible; she is ready to decide and to act. She has not abnegated power. But her definition of action, decision, and power is not heroic in the masculine sense. Her acts and choices do not involve ascendance, domination, power over others, and seem not to involve great consequences. They are "private" acts and choices, made in terms of immediate, actual relationships. To those who still believe that the public and the private can be separated, that there is a great world of men and war and politics and business and a little world of women and children and personal relations, and that these are truly worlds apart, one important, the other not—to such readers, Tenar's choice will appear foolish, and her story sadly unheroic.

Certainly, if we discard the axiom "What's important is done by men," with its corollary "What women do isn't important," then we've knocked a hole in the hero-tale, and a good deal may leak out. We may have lost quest, contest, and conquest as the plot, sacrifice as the key, victory or destruction as the ending; and the archetypes may change. There may be old men who aren't wise, witches who aren't wicked, mothers who don't devour. There may be no public triumph of good over evil, for in this new world what's good or bad, important or unimportant, hasn't been decided yet, if ever. Judgment is not referred up to the wise men. History is no longer about great men. The important choices and decisions may be obscure ones, not recognized or applauded by society.

Indeed, Ged's first heroic act, in *A Wizard of Earthsea,* was this kind of heroism, a personal choice almost unwitnessed and not sung about in the songs. But it was rewarded, and its reward was immediate: power. His power increased. He was on his way to becoming Archmage. In Tenar's Earthsea, there's neither acclaim nor reward; the outcomes of action are complex and obscure.

Perhaps it is this lack of applause, of "important," that has led some reviewers to state that all the men in *Tehanu* are weak or wicked. There are certainly a couple of very nasty villains, but *all* the men? Ogion? I suppose dying is a kind of weakness, but I thought he came through it rather well. As for the young king, he rescues Tenar from a persecutor, just as a hero should, and is clearly going to be an innovative and excellent statesman. Several women readers have objected fiercely that Tenar's son, Spark, is a selfish lout. Are all sons good, then, all wise, all generous? Tenar blames herself for Spark's weakness (just like a woman!), but I blame the society that spoiled the boy by giving him unearned power. After he's managed that farm a while alone, he'll probably shape up. Why do we expect more of the son than of the daughter?

But as for Ged, well, he has indeed lost his job. That's something we punish men for very cruelly. And when your job is being a hero, to lose it means you must indeed be weak and wicked.

In *Tehanu*, Ged's virtues are no longer the traditional male heroic ones: power as domination over others, unassailable strength, and the generosity of the rich. Traditional masculinists don't want heroism revised and unrewarded. They don't want to find it among housewives and elderly goatherds. And they really don't want their hero fooling around with grown women.

There never used to be any sex in Earthsea. My working title for *Tehanu* was *Better Late Than Never*.

Tenar always loved Ged, and knew it, but she can't figure out why she now, for the first time, desires him. Her friend the witch Moss explains it to her: Wizards give up one great power, sex, in order to get another, magic. They put themselves under a permanent spell of continence that affects everyone they have to do with. Why didn't I know that? Tenar says, and Moss cackles and explains that the magic of a really good spell is that you don't know it's working. It just "is," the way things "are." But when Ged lost his power as a mage, his spell of chastity went with it, and like it or lump it he's got his manhood back. The witch thinks this is funny.

Moss is a dirty old woman who's led a lively life. It seems that witches don't have to be chaste. They don't make the great sacrifice. Perhaps their powers are even nourished by their sexuality, but that's not clear. In fact, curiously little is known about witches in Earthsea, even by witches, even by the author. It looks as if the wizards have generally used their own powers in their own interests to keep their knowledge and skills from women. Women's work, as usual, is the maintenance of order and cleanliness, housekeeping, feeding and clothing people, childbearing, care of babies and children, nursing and healing of animals and people, care of the dying, funeral rites—those unimportant matters of life and death, not part of history, or of story. What women do is invisible. (Since they live without women, the wizards must do a lot of these invisible, "disappeared" things themselves, such as darning and dishwashing: a fact which I, like Moss, find funny. But pleasing, also. I was touched and delighted to discover that Ged was better at mending than I am.)

Old Moss is no revolutionary. She was taught that what men do is what matters. She supports this in her own devious way, saying "ours is only a little power, seems like, next to theirs. But it goes down deep. It's all roots. It's like an old blackberry thicket. And a wizard's power is like a fir tree, maybe, great and tall and grand, but it'll blow right down in a storm. Nothing kills a blackberry bramble." I'm afraid Moss is as essentialist as Allen Bloom. But because in this book the witch is allowed to speak, her mere presence subverts the tradition and its rules. If women can have both sex and magic, why can't men?

Continence; abstinence; denial of relationship. In the realm of male power, there is no interdependence of men with women. Manhood, according to Sigmund Freud, Robert Bly, and the hero-tale, is obtained and validated by the man's independence of women. The connection is severed. The heroic man's relation to women is limited to the artificial code of chivalry, which involves the adoration of a woman-shaped object. Women in that world are nonpeople, dehumanized by a beautiful, worshipful spell—a spell that may be seen, from the other side, as a curse.

A world in which men are seen as independently real and women are seen only as non-men is not a fantasy kingdom. It is every army. It's Washington, D.C. and the Tokyo Stock

Exchange. It's the corporate boardroom and the executive suite and the board of regents. It's the canon of English Literature. It's our politics. It's the world I lived in when I wrote the first three books of Earthsea. I lived under the spell, the curse. Most of us did, most of us do, most of the time. The myth of man alone, or alone with his God, at the center, on the top, is a very old, very powerful myth. It rules us still.

But thanks to the revisioning of gender called feminism, we can see the myth as a myth: a construct, which may be changed; an idea which may be rethought, made more true, more honest.

A rule may be unjust, yet its servants may be just. At the university Virginia Woolf could not enter, Tolkien taught. The mages of Roke were honest and just men, trying to use their power mindfully, keeping Equilibrium according to their lights. When she first came to Gont, Tenar lived as a student with a very wise mage, Ogion. Wouldn't he have taught her the uses of power? Well, we don't know if he would or not, because she refused. She quit grad school. She went off to be a nobody, a wife and mother. And now, as an aging widow not even allowed to own her farm, she's a sub-nobody. Was this a sacrifice? If so, what for?

Ged's bargain seems clearer. In the third book, he sacrifices his power, spending it to defeat a mortal evil. He triumphs, but at the cost of his heroic persona. As Archmage he is dead. And in *Tehanu* we find him weak, ill, depressed, forced to hide from enemies, at best a mere farmhand, good with a pitchfork. Readers who want him to be the Alpha Male are dismayed. They're dubious of a strength that doesn't involve contests and conquests and bossing people around.

Apparently it was the bossing around that Tenar refused, when she stopped studying with Ogion. Maybe Ogion, a maverick mage, would have shared his knowledge with her; but even if the wizardly hierarchy had accepted her, which seems doubtful, she evidently didn't want their kind of power. She wanted freedom.

She doesn't approve of sacrifice. "My soul can't live in that narrow place—this for that, tooth for tooth, death for life. . . . There is a freedom beyond that. Beyond payment, retribution, redemption—beyond all the bargains and the balances, there is freedom." And she didn't do any dying to get it. All her former selves are alive in her: the child Tenar, the girl-priestess Arha, who still thinks in Kargish, and Goha the farmwife, mother of two children. Tenar is whole, but not single. She is not pure. Just the opposite. She has borne, she has given birth to, her children and her new selves. She is not reborn, but rebearing. The word seems strange. We think of birth passively, as if we were all babies or all men. It takes an effort to think not of rebirth but of rebearing, actively, in the maternal mode: to think not as the apple but as the apple tree.

But what is Tenar's freedom? A very contingent thing. She lives alone; one night men surround her house, meaning to rape her and take her child from her. Victimized, she panics, she rushes from door to window; at last fear turns to rage, and seizing a knife she flings the door wide open. But it is Ged, playing the man's role to the hilt, who actually stabs one of the assailants. He has been gendered into violence, just as much as they have. And she has been gendered into mere response. Neither acts with genuine freedom, though they do act.

At the end of the book, both Ged and Tenar face the defenders of the old tradition. Having renounced the heroism of that tradition, they appear to be helpless. No magic, nothing they know, nothing they have been, can stand against the pure malevolence of institutionalized power. Their strength and salvation must come from outside the institutions and traditions. It must be a new thing.

Tenar's last child is one not born of her body, but given to her out of the fire, chosen by her soul. Raped, beaten, pushed into the fire, disfigured, one hand crippled, one eye blinded, this child is innocence in a different sense of the word. This is helplessness personified: disinheritance, a child dehumanized, made Other. And she was the key to this book. Until I saw Therru, until she chose me, there was no book. I couldn't see the story till I could look through her eye. But which eye, the seeing or the blind?

In a story I wrote not long before *Tehanu*, called *Buffalo Gals, Won't You Come Out Tonight?* a child called Myra survives a plane crash in the Oregon desert and is found by a coyote — that is, by Coyote, who created the world, according to the people there, and made quite a mess of it in the process. Myra has lost the sight of one eye in the crash. Some of Coyote's neighbors, Bluejay and Rattler and others, hold a dance and stick an eye made of pine pitch into the socket, and after Coyote licks it, it works fine. And Myra has a kind of double vision. She sees where the animals live not as burrows and dens but as a little village. She sees Coyote as a skinny woman in blue jeans with grayish blonde hair and a lot of no-good boyfriends, and she sees Horse as a beautiful long-haired man, and so on. And though the animals know she's human they see her as one of their own kind — Coyote sees her as a pup, Horse sees her as a filly, and Owl, who isn't paying much attention, sees her as an egg. But when Myra gets near where human beings live, she sees, with one eye, just a town like the one she grew up in, streets and houses and schoolkids. With the other eye, the new one, the wild one, she sees a terrifying hole in the fabric of the world — a noplace where time rushes like a torrent and everything is out of joint — Koyaanisqatsi. In the end she has to go back and live there, with her own people; but she asks Grandmother Spider if she can keep her new eye, and the Grandmother says yes. So maybe she will go on being able to see both worlds.

In *Tehanu*, Tenar is brushing her hair on a windy dry morning, so that it crackles and makes sparks, and the one-eyed child Therru is fascinated, seeing what she calls "The fire flying out all over the sky."

> At that moment Tenar first asked herself how Therru saw her—saw the world—and knew she did not know; that she could not know what one saw with an eye that had been burned away. And Ogion's words, *they will fear her,* returned to her; but she felt no fear of the child. Instead, she brushed her hair again, vigorously, so the sparks would fly, and once again she heard the little husky laugh of delight.

Soon after this scene, Tenar herself has a moment of double vision, seeing with two different eyes. An old man in the village has a beautiful painted fan; on one side are figures of lords and ladies of the royal court, but on the other side, usually hidden against the wall:

> Dragons moved as the folds of the fan moved. Painted faint and fine on the yellowed silk, dragons of pale red, blue, green moved and grouped, as the figures on the other side were grouped, among clouds and mountain peaks.
> "Hold it up to the light," said old Fan.
> She did so, and saw the two sides, the two paintings, made one by the light flowing through the silk, so that the clouds and peaks were the towers of the city, and the men and women were winged, and the dragons looked with human eyes.
> "You see?"

"I see," she murmured.

What is this double vision, two things seen as one? What can the blinded eye teach the seeing eye? What is the wilderness? Who are the dragons?

Dragons are archetypes, yes, mindforms, a way of knowing. But these dragons aren't St. George's earthy worm, nor are they the Emperor of China's airy servant. I am not European, I am not Asian, and I am not a man. These are the dragons of a new world, America, and the visionary forms of an old woman's mind. The mythopoeticists err, I think, in using the archetype as a rigid, filled mold. If we see it only as a vital potentiality, it becomes a guide into mystery. Fullness is a fine thing, but emptiness is the secret of it, as Lao Tze said. The dragons of Earthsea remain mysterious to me.

In the first three books, I think the dragons were, above all, wildness. What is *not owned*. A dragonlord wasn't a man who tamed dragons; nobody tamed dragons. He was simply, as Ged said, a man dragons would take notice of. But he couldn't look at them, not eye to eye. The rule was clear: A man must not look into a dragon's eyes.

In the first book we briefly met a young girl who wore a very small dragon on her wrist, like a bracelet; it had consented, temporarily, to be jewelry. Some tiny note was struck here that I remembered when, in the last book, Tenar meets a dragon, a full-scale one. She knows the rule, but then, she's not a man, is she? She and the dragon look at each other, eye to eye, and they know who they are. They recognize each other.

This echoes a legend told early in the book about the time when dragons and human beings were all one people, and how they became separated, and how they might yet be one.

And that legend brings into the European hero-tale tradition the great Native American mythos of the time when animals were people, the time of the making. Myra, the little Buffalo Gal in the Oregon desert, can live for a while in that Dream-time, that spiritual realm, because she's a child and a child adopted by a coyote, a wolfchild. Tenar doesn't live in it, but she connects with it—she can look the dragon in the eye—because she chose freedom over power. Her insignificance is her wild-ness. What she is and does is "beneath notice"—invisible to the men who own and control, the men in power. And so she's freer than any of them to connect with a different world, where things can be changed, remade. And the pledge of that connec-tion is, I think, her adoption of the child who has been destroyed by the irresponsible exercise of power, cast out of common humanity, made Other. Tenar is a wolfmother.

The dragon Kalessin in the last book is wildness seen not only as dangerous beauty but as dangerous anger. The fire of the dragon runs right through the book. It meets the fire of human rage, the cruel anger of the weak, which wreaks itself on the weaker in the endless circle of human violence. It meets that fire and consumes it, for "a wrong that cannot be repaired must be transcended." There's no way to repair or undo what was done to the child, and so there must be *a way to go on from there*. It can't be a plain and easy way. It involves a leap. It involves flying.

So the dragon is subversion, revolution, change—a going beyond the old order in which men were taught to own and dominate and women were taught to collude with them: the order of oppression. It is the wildness of the spirit and of the earth, uprising against misrule.

And it rejects gender.

Therru, the burned child, will grow up to be fully sexed, but she's been ungendered by the rape that destroys her "virtue" and the mutilation that destroys her beauty. She has nothing left of the girl men want girls to be. It's all been burned away. As for Ged and Tenar, they're fully sexed too, but on the edge of old age, when conventional gendering grants him some last flings and grants her nothing but modest grandmotherhood. And the dragon defies gender entirely. There are male and female dragons in the earlier books, but I don't know if Kalessin, the Eldest, is male or female or both or something else. I choose not to know. The deepest foundation of the order of oppression is gendering, which names the male normal, dominant, active, and the female other, subject, passive. To begin to imagine freedom, the myths of gender, like the myths of race, have to be exploded and discarded. My fiction does that by these troubling and ugly embodiments.

Oh, they say, what a shame, Le Guin has politicized her delightful fantasy world, Earthsea will never be the same.

I'll say it won't. The politics were there all along, the hidden politics of the hero-tale, the spell you don't know you're living under till you cast it off. At this conference, Jan Mark made the very simple and profound statement that the "world apart" of a fantasy inevitably refers back to this world. All the moral weight of it is real weight. The politics of Fairyland are ours.

With her wild eye, Myra sees the wilderness as well as the human realm as her true home. Therru, blinded, sees with the eye of the spirit as well as the eye of the flesh. Where does she see her home?

For a long time we've been seeing with only one eye. We've blinded the women's eye, said it doesn't see anything worth seeing, said all it can see is kids and cooking, said it's weak, short-sighted, said it's wicked, the evil eye. A woman's gaze is a fearful thing. It looks at a man, and he swells up "twice his natural size," and thinks he did it all himself. But then again the woman's eye looks at a hero and he shrinks. He shrinks right down to human size, man size, a fellow being, a brother, a lover, a father, a husband, a son. The woman looks at a dragon and the dragon looks right back. The free woman and the wild thing look at each other, and neither one wants to tame the other or own the other. Their eyes meet, they say each other's name.

I understand the mythology of *Tehanu* in this way: The child irreparably wronged, whose human inheritance has been taken from her—so many children in our world, all over our world now—that child is our guide.

The dragon is the stranger, the other, the not-human: a wild spirit, dangerous, winged, which escapes and destroys the artificial order of oppression. The dragon is the familiar also, our own imagining, a speaking spirit, wise, winged, which imagines a new order of freedom.

The child who is our care, the child we have betrayed, is our guide. She leads us to the dragon. She is the dragon.

While I was writing *Tehanu,* I didn't know where the story was going. I held on, held my breath, closed both eyes, sure I was falling. But wings upheld me, and when I dared look I saw a new world, or maybe only gulfs of sunlit air. The book insisted that it be written outdoors, in the sunlight and the open air. When autumn came and it wasn't done, still it would be written out of doors, so I sat in a coat and scarf, and the rain dripped off the verandah roof, and I flew. If some of the wild freedom of that flight is in the book, that's enough; that's how I wanted, as an old woman, to leave my beloved islands of Earthsea. I didn't want to leave Ged and Tenar and their dragon-child safe. I wanted to leave them free.

These remarks were made at *Worlds Apart,* CLNE at Oxford University, Oxford, England, in 1992.

METAPHORS TO LIVE BY

KATHERINE PATERSON

Rabbi Joseph Weizenbaum tells a story that he says came out of Israel some years ago. It seems that Henry Kissinger, on finding himself suddenly unemployed, sent his resume in to the Israeli government. After all, he reasoned, he'd done a lot for Israel, they ought to reciprocate. So they looked in the file and found out there was only one available job—curator of the Tel Aviv zoo. To their surprise, Henry took the job, and they forgot about him. Suddenly, one day, someone woke up and realized that nothing had been heard from their inexperienced if overqualified curator for months, so they sent an inspector around to see how he was doing. The inspector went down to the zoo and she saw that it was being perfectly cared for—if in a rather obsessive manner. The grounds were totally without litter. Every cage was scrubbed down to the bare concrete. The animals' coats were gleaming. Indeed, every blade of grass had been washed and blown dry. The inspector marveled as she went from aviary to the apes—from the bears to the bandicoots. At last she came to the lion cage and found it surrounded by a huge crowd of people. The inspector pushed her way through the crowd to the front. There in the cage was the great maned lion and lying next to him was a tiny white lamb. Henry himself was standing proudly in front of the cage. The inspector was overcome with awe. She took Kissinger to one side and said, "Henry, you have achieved the messianic dream: The lion and the lamb are lying down together. How did you accomplish that?"

"Veddy zimple," Henry says. "Effry morning, a fresh lamb."

I don't think I know how many speeches related to the theme of peace I've made over the years. It is my experience that while the lions keep changing, there's never any shortage. But finding a lamb that can make it through the day seems harder every time.

Part of the problem, I think, is that we've lived by the wrong metaphors. One of my closest friends from Norfolk days, Kathryn Morton, wrote me a note last fall to thank me for sending her a copy of *The King's Equal*. And since Kathryn turns a simple thank-you note into a literary masterpiece, the thanks led into a meditation upon the metaphors we live by.

She told me about a panel she had recently moderated where the panelists talked about children and literature.

"The panelists," she said, "had read their Bettelheim and supported the violence and contention we are used to in children's rhymes and stories, as though it were a necessity like salt on food. . . . Personally I have always wondered if the nursery rhymes and the Grimm versions aren't the happenstance that we have gotten stuck with, rather than being paragons or paradigms. We are stuck with railroad tracks built to the width of the Roman roads, impractically narrow now. We are stuck with dangerous, badly designed, top-heavy yellow school buses, made new every year in the same anachronistic mold. I try to envision children raised not on jingles about manic farmers wielding carving knives intent on mutilating mice. Instead, what would it be like if they read more rhymes as wise and salutary as *Yertle the Turtle*, for instance. . . ."

Then she goes on to talk about the power of language to

shape us. "What if," she asks, "what if we didn't use as the basic metaphor of group activity, sports, which are ritualized warfare, but if we used the choir as the standard metaphor for group activities—then we wouldn't come up with idiocies like 'My country right or wrong,' we'd think: 'A good descant makes the music richer.'"

To return to the guiding metaphor of this conference—plowshares demand more of us than swords. The work of peace is infinitely more difficult than the waging of war. For one thing we've had so little practice—not only little practice in peacemaking, but so little practice in imagining it.

If you look at the list of books you read for this institute, swords abound. We can imagine war. We, and I mean we writers, can write powerful, soul-wrenching books about it and its horrors. But when it comes to peace we are inarticulate. It's a truism that the snake has all the lines. That Lucifer is the hero we remember, not pale Adam. That without conflict we have no plot. But I think all that tells us is something tragic about ourselves. That when it comes to peace, our storied imaginations fail. We can't imagine what would be interesting enough about it to write a book.

If you learned history the way I did it was: There was this great heroic war—names of generals, dates of battles, place and date where the peace treaty or armistice was signed. Then nothing happened for X number of years until, suddenly, there was another great war—names of generals, dates of battle, place and date of treaty. Then X number of years in which nothing happened, until, whew, just in time, another great war—

Growing up in the South there was, of course, only one really great war. That one always puzzled me as a child. How, if the South had all the best generals and won all the big battles, did we manage to lose the war? It was never adequately explained. I tried to remember something that happened between wars in my history book, and the only thing I could come up with was the invention of the cotton gin. So there must have been a tip of the hat to the industrial revolution in the schools I attended—but there again, in order to give it any importance at all, we had to call it a "revolution."

We don't know what to do with peace. It's like happily ever after at the end of the fairy tale. Nothing happens after that. Now all of us, married or not, know that "they got married" is not the end of the story. Nor is the end of a particular war a happily ever after. We can hardly wait to get on to the next war so something will be happening.

We don't know how to make peace. We stand looking at the great, hulking machinery of war and we are paralyzed. How do we begin to beat *that* into instruments of peace? It's easier to look for a new enemy to aim at than to figure out how we can transform our submarines into shelters for the homeless and our bombers into well-baby clinics.

When I reread the passage in Isaiah which was the theme for this conference, I suddenly realized that I had been reading it wrong all my life. I had read the passage as though it was talking about the end of things—the happily ever after—after which, as we all know, nothing happens. Whereas, the prophet is saying that it's only after the swords are beaten into plowshares that the real productive work of life begins.

I took a close look at a plowshare in May. I was engaged in the making of a video that was to prove once again that I was real and alive. I'm quite good at proving both points. In fact I get more substantial every year. But this project was attempting a sort of *cinema verité*—or not very *verité*. I was to reenact some research that I had done in writing several of my books. This particular filming was done at the Shelburne Museum where I had indeed gone to do research, but for cinematic purposes, I was recreating a conversation with a member of the staff there that had never taken place, since I'd never met Garet Liver-more until after *Lyddie* was published. But the director thought a mid-nineteenth-century New England plow would make a good picture, so she had me asking Garet just how the plow would be used.

As Garet explained to me the angle at which I should hold the shafts, my mind jumped forward to tonight. Plows, I thought, demand much more of the user than swords. For one thing you couldn't use this plow by yourself. You needed a part-ner—a horse or ox or a strong family member to pull while another strong member held up the shafts and directed the point of the plowshare through the rocky New England soil. On particularly rough fields, you might need a third partner—a family member to walk by the head of the beast and guide it as it strained to pull the plow through the unfriendly soil. Now the writer who wrote these words in the book of Isaiah lived in an agricultural community. He knew that plowing was hard work. He never said recycle your swords into mobiles or sculp-tures or belt buckles, he said beat your swords into plow-shares—something that will make you work like a beast of burden but which will, in the long run, produce food for your family and your community. The same goes for spears. The only thing you do with a spear is skewer someone on it. But have you ever tried to trim a fruit tree? We've got a couple of old apple trees in our yard, so I've seen it done. It's hard work, potentially dangerous work, which is why I talked my husband out of doing it a second time. I got very nervous watching him climb that ladder and lean way out to lop off those dead or superflu-ous branches. But you have to do this if you want to make those trees produce—to be in the truest sense fruitful.

We haven't figured out, most of us, that peace is really hard work. We'd thought it was the happy ending. Remember the crumbling of the Berlin Wall? Before we'd really had a chance to celebrate we were confronted with neo-Naziism. Remember Yeltsin heroic on top of that tank? Before we could pop the champagne cork we were confronted with a society that simply disintegrated before our eyes. And what shall we say of Bosnia and Liberia and Cambodia and Somalia and Iraq and Sudan and Northern Ireland?

Finian O'Shea, whom many of you know, sent me a book of poems written by children from Northern Ireland.

This one by a six-year-old:

> Saint Patrick I know you help us in very many ways
> But now comes the time to help us in these days
> The fighting starts in Belfast
> And works its way to Dublin
> I'm afraid it's not snakes
> It's fighting that's our problem.

And this by a sixteen-year-old:

> They talk, the older folks,
> And paint a rosy past.
> Oh! I am tired of hearing
> How things were in Belfast.
>
> They talk and tell me stories
> Of the good times they once had.
> And the more they talk about it all
> The more it makes me sad.
>
> For I cannot remember
> A childhood free from strife,
> To me the bombs and bullets
> Are just a way of life.

> So I have just one question
> To ask our violent men.
> What about my wasted childhood,
> Can you bring it back again?

Libby Hofstetler at the Lion and the Lamb Peace Arts Center sent me these words, which accompanied children's artwork from Serbia:

> Yesterday my friend cried. He survived the hell. His mother, father, and his brother died in the war. Isn't it enough to stop that dirty war!
> We want our childhood spent in peace! Don't worry, be happy! I ask you: Why we, children, must live in war? Return me my smile, please. Stop the war. He is guilty for everything.

And from this nine-year-old:

> Have you a childrens? I don't want the war. I am sorry. . . . We are the children, listen to us because we are not guilty for this war.

As I was writing down these words from children caught up in war, I remembered a Lenten anthem we used to sing: *Listen to the lambs, all a-crying*—And suddenly the joke I told at the beginning of the speech turned very grim. The children of the world are the fresh lambs we supply every morning, noon, and night.

But what can we do? I don't know about you, but sometimes I feel that I'm just standing on the edge of the abyss wringing my hands.

When I was in Finland briefly in 1987, the tour guide was telling us about the Finnish language, which no one in the world except Finns speak. I may not remember this correctly, but my recollection is that in the Finnish language there are ninety-seven words to describe various degrees of drunkenness. Well, since then I've learned another Finnish word that we don't have a proper English translation for. The word is *sisu* and means, I'm told, a sort of spiritual toughness. Ah, I thought, that is what we lack, both the word and the quality. When it comes to making peace, we're a bunch of sissies. We have no degree of spiritual toughness. It takes *sisu* to beat swords into plowshares and more *sisu* to guide and pull the plows.

So where do we begin? Well, there is only one place we can begin and that is where we are. Let me amend that. There is only one place for me to begin and that is here in this room tonight.

I must look inside myself and discover the instruments of destruction that must be beaten into the instruments that work for life.

So I look inside and find—not despair exactly—but a hardening crust of cynicism. Surely not me? I am the great spy for hope? I looked up the word cynicism in the dictionary just to prove myself not guilty and this is what I found: cynic—a sneering faultfinder; one who doubts or denies the goodness of human motives, and who often displays his attitudes by sneers, sarcasm, etc.

Well, okay. So I doubt and deny the goodness of human motives. All we Calvinists do. We're realists, after all. Okay, so sometimes I've been caught sneering at certain former presidents, not to speak of vice presidents and current members of Congress and even certain benighted writers of so-called children's books. And maybe a few sarcastic words concerning those who seek to ban my beautiful books from the schools and libraries of this country have managed to slip through my clenched teeth. Is that cynicism? Surely not.

And then I remembered a story that I should never, ever

allow myself to forget. Some of you have heard this story before but I'm not going to let you forget it either.

It was the spring of 1975. We watched the television with growing horror as the years of fighting in South East Asia came down to Vietnamese clinging in vain to the ladders of escaping American helicopters and then on to the killing fields of Cambodia. And the children—always the suffering children. Some of them were snatched up out of the debacle and dumped parentless and bewildered into refugee camps.

Our own four children watched in horror. Their immediate, unanimous reaction was that we should adopt as many of these children as we could pack into our seven-room house. Now I would like to say that I was thrilled by my children's concern. Actually I was appalled. I was barely managing as the mother of four normal, happy, healthy children. Besides, I was in the middle of writing a book that was tearing me to pieces. Where was I supposed to summon up the sheer animal energy needed to feed and clean up after, not to speak of the psychic energy that would be demanded to care for and nurture, this small army of refugee children that my own four felt sure their mother would welcome with open arms?

Well, we compromised. We offered to be a temporary foster home for two Cambodian brothers who arrived with a group of children without parents or papers at Dulles Airport in May. We bought bunkbeds to turn the boys' room into a dormitory and I began cooking rice three times a day. For all my failings, I thought smugly, at least these boys have come to a home where the mother knows how to cook rice properly.

Well, I do know how to cook rice. That was never a problem. But rice was one of the few things that wasn't a problem. The days stretched into weeks and the weeks into nearly two months, and, although there were some exceptional incidents, on a day-to-day basis, my foster parent's lot was not a happy one.

What is the matter, I asked myself. Yes, the boys have problems, real problems, but I certainly had expected that. Yes, my own children are having difficulties accommodating, but come on, now, that was only to be expected. And then I realized that the real fault lay not in any of the children, homemade, adopted, or foster. The real fault lay in me. Whenever a problem arose, I was saying, "Well, we can't really deal with that. They're only going to be here a few days, weeks, months." Or: "Thank heavens, they're only going to be here a few days, weeks, months." And what I was doing was treating two human beings as though they were disposable.

Looking back, I'm not sure what I could or should have done differently, but I am sure that I should have thought differently. Because if anything is true, it is true that no human being is disposable. That every crime committed, every injustice permitted, every war that is waged goes back to this cynical assumption by one person or group of persons that another person or group of persons is disposable.

It is a cynicism I must constantly search out in my own heart and mind. But just to search it out is not enough. Guilt and despair do not make peace. The sword and spear must be utilized, they must be beaten into something that will be productive for life. So what can I make of this cynicism of mine? Perhaps it can be beaten into a pruning hook. The person who wields a pruning hook must be a realist. She must see what is harming growth and productivity and not be afraid to trim where needed, but the end result is life, not destruction. The spear of cynicism becomes a pruning hook—an instrument of imaginative judgment.

I've been reading a book about children's war play titled *Who's Calling the Shots?* In it the authors, Diane Levine and Nancy Carlsson-Paige, make the point that while it is almost impossible to stop children playing war, adults can help children turn war play into a productive imaginative activity. The problem with war toys, they say, especially those hawked in half-hour commercials in children's TV programs, is that they lead to imitative violence rather than imaginative play. I think these women are on to something. They never say to parents, "Stop all war games"; rather they show how those games may help a child evolve beyond aggression. So while most of us are sneering cynically at Saturday morning cartoons, produced by cynical toy merchants who consider money valuable and children disposable, these writers are showing parents who have to live in the real world how to beat cynicism into imaginative play that will help rather than harm their children. I would be interested in other people's reactions to this book. I was impressed.

Okay. What else, what else is down there in that murky psyche? Well, there's envy. No, surely not. Who could I be envious of? Hah! I'm not naming names tonight, some of them are sitting here tonight a bit close for comfort, but if you think for one moment that I am envy-free you haven't read *Jacob Have I Loved*. It would be nice to think that writing that book cured me of that particular sin, but the best I can say is that it made me confront it rather baldly. Suffice it to say, I recognize and continue to recognize the sword of envy. Envy cuts both ways. The sharpest edge cuts toward the envious one. A. S. Byatt writing in the *New York Times Book Review* section, in the series on the Seven Deadly Sins, quotes the Wisdom of Solomon, which says "Through envy of the devil came death into the world." Of course, this is the theme of *Paradise Lost*, Lucifer's envy, which brings Adam and Eve to sin. It is envy that causes Cain to kill his brother Abel. It is envy that blinds and hobbles Louise, that prods Iago and twists Uriah Heap.

There is a terrible corrosive quality to envy, all the more so, as Byatt reminds us, because there is a kinship between envy and justice. The small child cries out, "It's not fair!" demanding that the universe be just. But as most of us remember telling our outraged children, "Life is not fair." It is not the nature of the created world to be just. The only creature who expects or demands justice is the one created in the image of God. For better and often times for worse the work of justice has been entrusted to human beings.

My friend Kathryn Morton tells of a Jewish prayer in which you say, "What is it for us to do? It is for us to heal the world." This prayer, called the *Tikkun Olam*, comes from the mystical aspect of the Jewish tradition. "The story," says Kathryn, "is that there was an original great light and it was divided and spread and cast all asunder and it is for each of us (who has a part of the light inside themselves) to gather more, to gather the light back together, and when the light is all reunited, it will be the coming of the Messiah—heaven on earth. I'm not much into mysticism," Kathryn says, "but I think it's a wonderful metaphor. . . . It's a metaphor I can live by."

So part of the work of peace is gathering of light or, to go back to our original metaphor, the beating of the sword of envy into the plowshare of justice. It's not just doing what comes naturally. It demands a whole new way of looking at ourselves and our fellows. We must turn from the childish demand for fairness for ourselves and turn toward the vision of justice for everyone.

At Saint Michael's four summers ago, many of you heard Tom Feelings give one of the most powerful speeches I have ever heard one of my colleagues give. In that speech Tom quoted President Jimmy Carter in a statement that I have gone over and over in my head since I first heard it.

Mr. Carter said,

> There is still an element of racism that is inherent
> in perhaps all of us. I try not to be a racist and
> wouldn't call myself a racist, but I have feelings

that border on it. And that is embarrassing to me sometimes. When the TV screens were filled with little Ethiopian and Sudanese children walking along with distended bellies and dying in the arms of their dying mothers, it's hard for me to believe that one of these children, in the eyes of God, is as important as Amy, my daughter. How many of these little black kids does it take to equal one Amy? Fifteen? Twenty? Ten? Five? I think the answer is one. But it's hard for me to believe this. I think all of us to some degree are guilty of an insensitivity to the needs and ideas of others.

In the arithmetic of justice, my friends, one must always equal one.

Perhaps the most troubling phrase to come out of the Gulf War was the oft-repeated sentence of our leaders: "Thank God there was so little loss of life." And yet we know that 100,000 men, women, and children died in that war. A woman in Ohio has made a mural with 100,000 faces on it. It takes a long time, my friends, to walk past 100,000 faces.

As Barbara Harrison reminded you earlier this week, the sword and plowshares metaphor occurs more than once in the Bible. The prophet Micah uses it to portray the Messianic ideal, but he adds a verse that I find significant. Let me read again Micah's addition to the now familiar words of swords and plowshares:

But they shall sit every man under his vine and under his fig tree, and none shall make them afraid; for the mouth of the Lord of hosts has spoken.

For all the peoples walk each in the name of
its god, but we will walk in the name of the Lord
our God for ever and ever.

Justice for the Hebrews meant not only turning the instruments of war into the tools necessary for productive life, but
making sure that all persons have their own productive space —
where they can live and work totally without threat. They can
even worship any gods they choose. "And none shall make them
afraid." So let me say as an aside something that should never
be thought of as an aside — that the Messianic vision is totally
inclusive. No one is disposable. Everyone's individual home and
work and for that matter religion is respected. Wow, if we could
only plant that vision in Cambodia and Northern Ireland and
the Middle East and the United States.

Well, we have only one place we can begin and that is with
ourselves tonight in this room. But to do this we need to beat
our own cynicism, our own envy, and yes, our own fears into
instruments of life.

Thomas Jefferson has a tattered reputation in our day.
Much has been made of his maintaining a black mistress and
speaking out for freedom while remaining a slave owner. Which
leads to the accusation of hypocrisy which, as all us righteous
people know, is the worst crime anyone could be accused of.

In the book by Fawn Brodie, *Thomas Jefferson: An Intimate
History*, the author writes:

> When Jefferson wrote that all men were created
> equal and entitled to life, liberty and the pursuit
> of happiness, he was enunciating an ideal as if it
> were a reality. This was one of Jefferson's special
> qualities as a revolutionary statesman: that he
> could define the visionary future as if it were the
> living present. . . . There was no contradiction

when he said "It is so," and meant "It will be so."
It was not the melancholy of his great burdens
but the vision of what could be that held him. He
would not let faith in his own destiny be
destroyed by what was. . . .

As I read these words I remembered the prophet Jeremiah
who had prophesied the destruction of his nation while being
scorned as a fool and imprisoned as a traitor. Then, finally, the
worst of his prophesies were about to come true, the city was
about to fall, and he was in jail for uttering treason. Instead of
saying "I told you so," Jeremiah sent his assistant Baruch out
to buy a piece of land. Yes, the land would be overrun by the
enemy, yes, the city would be destroyed and the inhabitants
would be taken away to live as exiles in Babylon. But Jeremiah
had the deeds to his property put in an earthenware vessel "that
they may last for a long time. For thus says the Lord of hosts,
the God of Israel: Houses and fields and vineyards shall again
be brought in this land."

Perhaps some of you have seen the *Time* magazine of July
26. In it are a group of pictures that had been taken on black-
market film and sent out of Sarajevo through enemy lines. The
pictures were taken by a Bosnian photographer determined to
document for the world the suffering of his people. They are
pictures of utter desolation and despair—with one startling
exception. Two hospital beds have been pushed together. On
the beds are a young man and a young woman, their arms
entwined. There is a bouquet on her bed and a large sign hung
at the foot of each bed. Her sign reads "Just" and his reads
"Married." The caption beneath the picture reads: "Eternal
Optimism: A couple who both lost legs to Serbian shells bet on
the future."

This is not eternal optimism. In the self-declared "city without hope" this is hope worthy of a Jefferson or a Jeremiah.

In closing, I want to share a swords and plowshares story from my own family history. Among old letters, I found some that my father as a young man had written home from France. He returned with one leg and gas in his lungs, but that's another story. As a student my father became a part of the volunteer ambulance corps, recruited from American colleges and universities to serve with the French army. Perhaps you remember another of those young men—Ernest Hemingway.

The letter is dated July 28, 1918, and tells of the Second Battle of the Marne. My father was twenty-four years old, driving a T-Model Ford ambulance, fondly nicknamed a Tin Lizzy.

Just a part of the letter:

> The souvenir gatherers should be here. They could find anything from a [German] tank to cartridges and the like. I have seen so many helmets, etc., that I would like to get to a place where there are no souvenirs. You have seen the pictures of the forests, how they are torn and ruined; well, those are no exaggerations. I saw this afternoon one tree between three and four feet in diameter cut off. And the smaller trees are lying in a tangled heap everywhere. Now and then there will be a shell that did not explode in a tree, while some of the trees are so full of shrapnel and bullets that they are well loaded.
>
> We are well. Our headquarters are in a small town where it was impossible to find enough of a good roof left to keep the cooking stove dry. So you see we must sleep in our cars or in dugouts, which are very damp, especially after several rainy days that we have had. Such is life in a place that wherever you and your "Lizzy" keep

together you are at home. You never worry
about getting back, you are always there.

And then, almost as an afterthought, he adds these words:

The wheat, what is left, is very fine indeed, if it
could be harvested.

The letter ends there, but not the story. A friend in my
father's ambulance division, the only Yankee to be placed
among the Washington and Lee University volunteers, tells in
his memoirs what happened a few days later.

There was a lull in the fighting and my father came to him.
"See that field of wheat," he asked. "There's only an old couple
living on that farm. There's no one left strong enough to bring
in a crop of that size. It would be a shame to let it go to waste."

So the two of them, Virginia farm boy and Wisconsin school
teacher, borrowed scythes and harvested the field of ripe grain
before the next battle could destroy it.

This, as my friend Kathryn Morton would say, is a
metaphor I can live by.

These remarks were made at *Swords and
Ploughshares*, CLNE at Harvard University, Cambridge, Massachusetts, in 1993.

BIOGRAPHIES

GILLIAN CROSS is the author of more than thirty books, some of which have been adapted for the screen and shown on Children's BBC television. She has won three major British awards for her work: In 1990 she was winner of the Library Association's Carnegie Medal for *Wolf*, and in 1992 *The Great Elephant Chase* was the winner of the Whitbread Children's Novel Award and the overall winner of the Smarties Prize. In between and alongside all these things, she has worked as an unqualified teacher in a primary school (when she was nineteen), as an assistant to a village baker (when she was twenty-three), as a nanny (when she was about thirty), and as an assistant to a Member of Parliament (when she was about thirty-two). She now lives in Warwickshire, in the middle of England, with her husband and their two younger children.

SHARON CREECH was awarded the 1995 Newbery Medal for *Walk Two Moons*. She is also the author of *Absolutely Normal Chaos; Chasing Redbird; Pleasing the Ghost;* and *Bloomability*. After nearly twenty years teaching and writing in Europe, Sharon Creech has recently returned to the United States to live.

PHOTO: MATTHEW SELF

MAURICE SENDAK has created or illustrated more than seventy-five children's books. In 1964 he received the Caldecott Medal for *Where the Wild Things Are.* In 1970 he became the first American illustrator to receive the international Hans Christian Andersen Medal, given in recognition of his entire body of work. His works include illustrations for *The Juniper Tree and Other Tales from Grimm* and

PHOTO: MICHAEL COOPER

Dear Mili, a newly discovered tale by Wilhelm Grimm, and children's books by Else Holmelund Minarik, Randall Jarrell, and Isaac Bashevis Singer.

Mr. Sendak is also noted as a designer of stage sets and costumes for operas, including Mozart's *Die Zauberflöte* and *Idomeneo,* Janácek's *The Cunning Little Vixen,* and Prokofiev's *L'Amor des Trois Orange.* His costumes and design for Tchaikovsky's *The Nutcracker* ballet became the basis of a successful feature film.

Several of Mr. Sendak's books have been adapted for television and theater, including *The Sign on Rosie's Door* and *The Nutshell Library,* which became the basis for *Really Rosie,* an animated television special and an Off-Broadway musical. In 1990, with Arthur Yorinks, he founded The Night Kitchen, a national theater company devoted to the development of quality productions for children. In 1997, Mr. Sendak received an honorary Doctor of Letters degree from Yale University and the National Medal of Arts from President Clinton.

SARAH ELLIS is a Vancouver writer, librarian, story-teller, and book reviewer. She has lectured on children's literature in Japan, Ireland, and the United States. Her books include *A*

Family Project, a Horn Book Fanfare List book; *Pick-Up Sticks,* winner of the Governor General's Award; and *Out of the Blue,* winner of the Mr. Christie Book Prize. Her latest book, *Back of Beyond,* won the Sheila Egoff Prize. In 1999 she takes temporary leave of her wet West Coast home to be Writer-in-Residence at the University of Toronto.

PHOTO: ANDY NEWMAN

GREGORY MAGUIRE is the author of over a dozen novels for children, including *Missing Sisters; The Good Liar;* and *The Hamlet Chronicles.* His work for adults includes *Wicked: The Life and Times of the Wicked Witch of the West* and *Confessions of an Ugly Stepsister.* He holds a doctorate in English and American literature from Tufts University, and he has taught at several Boston-area colleges, but he prefers his stints as writer-in-residence or visiting author in schools as far afield as north Dublin, south Boston, Nairobi, and Hollywood. Gregory Maguire has written for the *Horn Book Magazine,* the *Christian Science Monitor,* and the *New York Times Book Review.* He is a codirector and founding board member of Children's Literature New England, and he lives in Concord, Massachusetts.

PHOTO: PAUL SCHNECK PHOTOGRAPHY

SUSAN COOPER is a novelist and screenwriter whose books include *The Boggart* and *The Boggart and the Monster;* the fantasy sequence *The Dark Is Rising;* and a collection of essays on children's literature entitled *Dreams and Wishes.* She has won the Newbery Medal and the Boston Globe–Horn Book Award and twice been runner-up for the Carnegie Medal. Born in England, she has two children and lives in Connecticut.

PAT O'SHEA grew up in Galway in the 1930s in a community that was warm and generous to children and where friendships between the very young and very old were commonplace. The Irish tradition of story-telling by the fireside (especially in wintertime), for the pleasure of children and adults alike, still prevailed. There was a magic in that, in the atmosphere created and in gazing into the fire, and in the vividness of the stories themselves. This magic made her want, when she came to writing *The Hounds of the Morrigan,* to create something that would be of comparable intensity and vividness in the imaginations of the children reading it. In her writing Ms. O'Shea draws extensively on her idyllic childhood. In 1947, at the age of sixteen, she went to England for a holiday and is still there.

BETTY LEVIN has taught literature, children's literature, history, and creative writing to high school students, undergraduates, and graduate students. She was a founding member of the board of Children's Literature New England. Her twenty books for young readers include *Brother Moose; Gift Horse;* and *The Trouble with Gramary* (winner of the Judy Lopez Award). *Away to Me, Moss* won a Parents' Choice Award. More recent titles include *Look Back, Moss; Creature Crossing;* and *The Banished.* Ms. Levin lives in Lincoln, Massachusetts, where she raises Border Leicester sheep and working sheep dogs. Her three grown children still sometimes help on the farm.

PHOTO: KYLE BAJAKIAN

* * *

TOM FEELINGS has focused on African culture and the Black American experience throughout his distinguished career. *Soul Looks Back in Wonder,* whose award-winning art was exhibited at the Schomburg Center for Black Culture in New York City, has original poems by Maya Angelou and Margaret Walker, among others, as well as a previously unpublished poem by Langston Hughes. Mr. Feelings collaborated with Maya Angelou on *Now Sheba Sings the Song.* Born and raised in Brooklyn, New York, he attended the School of Visual Arts and later lived in Ghana, West Africa, and in Guyana, South America. He is the recipient of a grant from the National Endowment for the Arts, and is a retired professor of art at the University of South Carolina at Columbia. His magnum opus, *The Middle Passage,* was published in 1995.

JOHN ROWE TOWNSEND was born in Leeds, England, and went to Leeds Grammar School and Cambridge University, where he received an honors degree in English. For many years he was a journalist on the (formerly *Manchester*) *Guardian.* He has published more than twenty books, mostly for children and young people, and edited an Oxford poetry anthology. His history of English-language children's literature, *Written for Children,* is currently in its sixth edition in the United States and Britain. He is an adjunct board member of Children's Literature New England.

*   *   *

MADELEINE L'ENGLE has been an actress, a poet, a playwright, and an essayist. She is the renowned author of *A Wrinkle in Time*, winner of the Newbery Medal, and over fifty books for children and adults, including *Meet the Austins; A Wind in the Door; A Swiftly Tilting Planet; A Ring of Endless Light*, a Newbery Honor Book; and *An Acceptable Time*. She is the

PHOTO: SIGRID ESTRADA

recipient of the Regina Medal for "distinguished dedication to children's literature." In 1998, for achievement in writing for young adults, Madeleine L'Engle received the Margaret Edwards Award from the American Library Association.

Ms. L'Engle is the Writer-in-Residence at the Cathedral of Saint John the Divine in New York City.

VIRGINIA HAMILTON is the celebrated author of both fiction and nonfiction. For *M. C. Higgins, the Great* she received three major honors: the Newbery Medal, the National Book Award, and the Boston Globe–Horn Book Award. Virginia Hamilton is also the author of *The Planet of Junior Brown* and *Arilla Sun Down*. For *Sweet Whispers, Brother Rush* and *The People Could Fly: American Black Folk*

PHOTO: JIMMY BYRGE

Tales, she was given the Coretta Scott King Award. She is the recipient of the Boston Globe–Horn Book Award for *In the Beginning: Creation Stories from Around the World*. Ms. Hamilton has received the international Hans Christian Andersen Medal. She was the winner of the 1995 Laura Ingalls Wilder Medal, and is the first children's writer to be awarded a John D. and Catherine T. MacArthur Foundation grant. Her recent novels include *Second Cousins* and *Plain City*.

PHOTO: JOHN ROWE TOWNSEND

JILL PATON WALSH was born in London on April 29, 1937, and went to Saint Michael's Convent, North Finchley, and Saint Anne's College, Oxford. From 1959 to 1962 she taught English at Enfield Girls' Grammar School. She has written many children's novels, including *Unleaving* and *Grace,* and several picture books. She has contributed articles and reviews to many journals and is an adjunct board member of Children's Literature New England. More recently she has written for adults; in 1994 her novel *Knowledge of Angels* was short-listed for the Booker Prize. In 1996 she received the CBE for services to literature and was elected a fellow of the Royal Society of Literature. In 1998 her children's novel *A Chance Child* won the Phoenix Award.

PHOTO: MAGGIE STERN TERRIS

BARBARA HARRISON is the author with Daniel Terris of *A Twilight Struggle: The Life of John Fitzgerald Kennedy* and *A Ripple of Hope: The Life of Robert F. Kennedy. Theo,* her forthcoming novel for young people, is set in war-torn Greece at the height of the Nazi occupation. She is also the author of reviews and essays on reading, literature, and contemporary society published in *Commonweal,* the *Horn Book Magazine,* and the *Quarterly Journal of the Library of Congress,* and coeditor of *Innocence and Experience: Essays and Conversations on Children's Literature.* She was the founding director of the Center for the Study of Children's Literature at Simmons College. She teaches English in Newton, Massachusetts, and is codirector of Children's Literature New England. She grew up in Washington, D.C., and currently lives in Cambridge, Massachusetts.

MARGARET MAHY is the author of over forty novels, poetry collections, and picture books, including *The Tricksters; The Three-Legged Cat; Dangerous Spaces; The Catalogue of the Universe; The Other Side of Silence; Underrunners; Memory;* and *Bubble Trouble and Other Poems.* Twice she won the Carnegie Medal in England, in 1982 for *The Haunting* and in 1984 for *The Changeover: A Supernatural Romance.*

She lives in a New Zealand village in the crater of an extinct volcano, trying to write books of her own and to read as many as possible of other people's. At the moment, in May 1998, Margaret has a standard poodle, two cats, two daughters, and three and a half grandchildren. She struggles with computers and tries to prevent herself from disappearing under an inexorable avalanche of paper. She talks a lot—sometimes to the dog and often to herself. Her best books are still lost in her head, trying to break free but never quite succeeding.

URSULA K. LE GUIN, born in California in 1929, lives in Oregon; she has received many academic, popular, and literary awards for her more than forty books of fiction, poetry, criticism, and children's stories. *A Wizard of Earthsea* received the Boston Globe–Horn Book Award, *The Tombs of Atuan* the National

PHOTO: MARIAN WOOD KALISCH

Book Award, and *Tehanu* the Nebula Award. Her most recent books are a translation of Lao Tzu's *Tao Te Ching,* and a workbook on story-writing, *Steering the Craft.*

"Earthsea Revisioned" appeared as a pamphlet published in 1993 by Green Bay Publications, Cambridge, England, in collaboration with Children's Literature New England.

PHOTO: SAMANTHA LOOMIS PATERSON

KATHERINE PATERSON is the author of more than twenty-five books, including twelve novels for young people. Two of these novels are National Book Award Winners, *The Master Puppeteer,* 1977, and *The Great Gilly Hopkins,* 1979. She also received the Newbery Medal in 1978 for *Bridge to Terabithia* and again in 1981 for *Jacob Have I Loved.* Her latest novel is *Jip, His Story,* the winner of the 1997 Scott O'Dell Award for Historical Fiction.

In addition to her novels, she is the author of two collections of Christmas stories; a collection of essays on reading and writing books for children; *Parzival,* a retelling of Wolfram's romantic epic; translations of Japanese picture books; story books; and various articles and reviews for journals and newspapers, including the *Washington Post* and the *New York Times.* Her books have been published in twenty-two languages, and she is the 1998 recipient of the international Hans Christian Andersen Medal.

Mrs. Paterson was born in China of missionary parents, coming to the United States at the start of World War II. She is a graduate of King College, Bristol, Tennessee, the Presbyterian School of Christian Education in Richmond, Virginia, and Union Theological Seminary in New York City. She is married to the Reverend John B. Paterson, a Presbyterian pastor, with whom she has written two books, *Consider the Lilies: Plants of the Bible* and *Images of God.* The Patersons have four children and four grandchildren